Banners in the Air

Curtis V. Hard. (Courtesy of the Stark County Historical Society, Canton, Ohio.)

Banners in the Air

The Eighth Ohio Volunteers and the Spanish-American War

by Curtis V. Hard

edited by Robert H. Ferrell

THE KENT STATE UNIVERSITY PRESS

Kent, Ohio, and London, England

Library of Congress Catalog Card Number 88-12033
ISBN 0-87338-367-2
Manufactured in the United States of America

Unless otherwise noted, photographs are reproduced through the courtesy of Ellen Palmer Bliss and Priscilla M. Harding.

Library of Congress Cataloging-in-Publication Data

Hard, Curtis V., 1845-1917.
Banners in the air: the Eighth Ohio Volunteers and the Spanish-American War / by Curtis V. Hard; edited by Robert H. Ferrell.
p. cm.
Bibliography: p.
Includes index.
ISBN 0-87338-367-2 (alk. paper)
1. Hard, Curtis V., 1845-1917. 2. United States. Army. Ohio Volunteers, Eighth—Biography. 3. United States—History—War of 1898—Personal narratives. 4. Ohio—History—War of 1898—Personal narratives. 5. Soldiers—Ohio—Biography. I. Ferrell, Robert H. II. Title.
E726.03H37 1988 88-12033
973.8'98—dc19 CIP

British Library Cataloguing-in-Publication data are available.

Contents

Preface

Curtis V. Hard, the author of the memoir that follows, of the Eighth Ohio Volunteers during the Spanish-American War, spent most of his life in Wooster, Ohio, where he was born in 1845 and died in 1917. The colonel's father was a minister. The family had come from Vermont. As a youth Hard served in the Civil War; in 1864 he enlisted in the 135th Regiment of Ohio Volunteers and fought with Sheridan's army in the Shenandoah. After the war he became a bookkeeper and eventually cashier of the National Bank of Wooster. In later years his business interests included the "interurban" that ran between Wooster and Cleveland, the Cleveland and Wooster Electric Railway, and he was a promoter of another such line from Cleveland to Ashland and Mansfield. He organized and was the manager and largest stockholder of the Wooster Electric Company, and was president of the Cleveland Light and Power Company. He married Mary Adaline Jackson in 1871, and they had three daughters and a son, Dudley J.—who served in the regiment as a lieutenant in 1898, became a colonel of artillery during World War I, and held a commission as a major general in the Ohio National Guard during the 1930s.

It was in the papers of Curtis Hard's son, Dudley, in the Western Reserve Historical Society in Cleveland, that I found the memoir of the Eighth Ohio in 1898. Dudley Hard had arranged to have the manuscript typed, but never did anything further with it.

There are several reasons for bringing this account into print. For one, it is very nicely written—indeed, strikingly so. Any college teacher accustomed to misspellings and sentence fragments and other student errors too numerous to mention will delight in discovering that a man of long ago, with limited education, could write so well (after the Civil War, Hard entered nearby Berea College, which was later Baldwin-Wallace, but soon returned to Wooster, never graduating).

Moreover, Hard clearly and forcefully tells what he saw. The reader easily acquires a feeling for army life during the last war of the nineteenth century. The colonel of the Eighth Ohio describes a series of human predicaments, tasks presenting themselves. If their solutions nominally followed out of a few army regulations, they came mainly, as he recognized, out of common sense, that resort of all good soldiers. The memoir does unconsciously set out the patriotism of the time, some of which will seem excessive. No longer can Americans think of going to war with banners in the air. Apart from a few such commentaries Hard's account holds remarkably to description of war "as it was."

A third reason for publishing this memoir of the Spanish-American War is that the subject itself, the war of 1898, is of high importance for American history in the present century. In 1898 the country's foreign relations "came of age." The war constituted a departure, an understanding that older ways would no longer work, that the foreign policy of Washington and Jefferson and Monroe lay in the distant past. The United States had become the world's principal industrial power. New ways of communication—steamships, railroads, telegraphs, cables, telephones—were bringing the nations together. It was the end of isolation. All this was captured by the French phrase then fashionable, usually referring to literary and architectural change, about a "fin de siècle." The country could no longer escape what Washington had described in 1796 as the extraordinary combinations and collisions of the nations of Europe. During and after World War II, Americans discovered that they also would have to reckon with extraordinary combinations and collisions in Asia.

For manuscripts, including the memoir itself, I am much indebted to the staff of the Western Reserve Historical Society. In the beginning it was a pleasure to work in the clutter of the old library, then in the one-time mansion that contains the society's offices and museum; now everything is up-to-date in the new library building constructed behind the mansion.

I am beholden to the curators and trustees and secretaries of the county and city historical societies of Northeastern Ohio, who answered queries and for the most part confessed they held no records that pertained to the Eighth Ohio Volunteers. Of considerable use, however, were the holdings of the Stark County Historical Society in Canton, whose director, Richard E. Werstler, extended every courtesy. My meeting with Dick Werstler, I might add, was oddly memorable. Driving into the parking lot of his society's building, which stands next to the McKinley Memorial, I espied a lithe figure running up the grassy slope toward the memorial's entrance, where the great bronze door stood open. A sign at the bottom of the memorial's steps related that the building was closed for the winter. I followed Dick into the rounded hall containing the caskets of William and Ida McKinley, discernible in the winter gloom, and met him down a side staircase where he was testing the lights in anticipation of a reconstruction of the dilapidated structure.

John Miller of the American History Research Center of the University of Akron made available interesting material, including the only diary by a member of the Eighth that has survived. The university library has microfilm runs of the *Akron Beacon Journal* (sometimes the *Summit County Beacon*).

The staff of the Ohio Historical Society in Columbus was most helpful, as always. The society possesses the papers of Lieutenant Colonel Charles W. F. Dick and Governor Asa S. Bushnell, together with the records of the state adjutant general.

Richard J. Sommers of the U.S. Army Military History Institute at Carlisle Barracks provided the diary of Brigadier General Adelbert Ames, who accompanied the Eighth to Cuba, and also a long letter by a young soldier to his father describing the trip from Camp Bushnell near Columbus to Camp Alger near Washington, D.C., the only item of importance on the Eighth in the army's archives.

William E. Lind of the Military Archives Division of the National Archives arranged for copies of Colonel Hard's compiled service records and also those of Lieutenant Colonel Dick.

Many photographs of interest were in an album belonging to Colonel Hard's son Dudley and others were in an album of Brigadier General George A. Garretson. Both albums are in the Western Reserve Historical Society. The library's photo-archivist, Michael McCormick, helped with selection as well as production from these albums. Frank Klein of The Bookseller, in Akron, possessed a remarkable stereograph slide, and kindly lent it for reproduction. Thanks, too, to Michael J. Winey of the Military History Institute at Carlisle, and for the expert photography of Colonel Jim Enos. And my thanks also to the staffs of the Library of Congress and the National Archives, the former for an admirable group of stereographs, the latter for three good photographs. Sometimes one discovery leads to another, and a National Archives photograph, unindexed but with a tell-tale "8 Reg." penciled on the back, together with a date, established Adelbert Ames, Jr., as the photographer, and led to fifty photos in his father's papers in the Sophia Smith Collection of the Smith College Archives in Northampton, Massachusetts. For help with that collection I am much indebted to Susan Boone.

But the best photographs of the Eighth Ohio Volunteers were taken by chief musician William R. Palmer, bandmaster of the Eighth. I am grateful to his grand-niece and granddaughter, Priscilla M. Harding and Ellen Palmer Bliss, for allowing access to the Palmer album, now in Mrs. Bliss's possession.

It has been a pleasure working with Lynne McCaffry, who knows how to track down difficult items in the library; with John M. Hollingsworth, a first-rate cartographer; and with members of the departments of history at the University of Akron and at Kent State—George W. Knepper and the late Warren F. Kuehl at Akron, Lawrence S. Kaplan and John T. Hubbell at Kent. To John and his able staff at the Kent State University Press, especially to managing editor Julia Morton, a special thanks.

R. H. F.

Editorial Note

The pages that follow publish virtually the entire manuscript of Colonel Hard, with the exception of preliminaries in which he recited orders and supplementary advice received from Columbus and Washington prior to mustering the regiment, and an exhaustive description of rations during the voyage home on the *Mohawk*. Because the colonel wrote not merely with clarity but grammatical care, it has only been necessary to make such minor changes as insertion of commas, turning of semicolons to colons or commas, and conversion of written-out numbers to Arabic. Like all the Victorians, Hard was fond of capitalizations, and they are gone. Military unit designations conform to later practice, such as Eighth Regiment or 7th Battalion. Some of the telegrams, cables, and newspaper accounts that he inserted in his text are now in the notes.

Introduction

The cause of the Spanish-American War was the revolutionary situation in Cuba, the revolt against Spanish rule that broke out in 1895, which led to American intervention. To be sure, the American people were in a mood for war, and for the rewards of war. which in a war with Spain would mean the accession of imperial territories. The new Darwinian philosophy that had taken hold in the United States almost called for empire; it divided the peoples of the world into inferior and superior nations, with the Anglo-Saxons—the Americans, British, and Germans—possessing the most superior national attributes. Beginning in the early 1880s the United States constructed a new navy of steel and steam and rifled guns, replacing its aging ships of wood and sail and smoothbore cannon, and the very existence of these new ships by the end of the century created a temptation to use them. Moreover, a series of opportunities for demonstrating national prowess had presented themselves: involvement in the Samoan Islands, in the Hawaiians, in a contention with the government of Chile over an attack upon a shore party of American sailors in the port of Valparaíso, and lastly an assertion of the Monroe Doctrine against Great Britain over the boundary between Venezuela and British Guiana. All these developments had been moving the American nation toward war. But it was the Cuban revolution that persuaded President William McKinley and his countrymen that the time for war had arrived.

The revolt in Cuba had been many years, by some measurements nearly a century, in coming. During the Napoleonic Wars all of Spain's colonies in the New World had revolted and obtained independence, save Cuba and Puerto Rico. For some reason the revolutionary infection, the ideas of such New World patriots as Simon Bolívar, did not immediately affect Cuba. Possibly it was because Cuba was an island. Perhaps because many of the people of

Cuba were of Spanish descent, or somehow felt they were closer to the culture of Spain. A revolution did not break out until after the American Civil War, when perhaps the ideas of liberty more easily came to Cuba, or maybe it was because a junta established itself in New York City. The revolt that began in 1868 achieved some small successes, but eventually wound down and ended ten years later without any change in Cuba's status. Then another revolution broke out, and it was this second uprising that led to American intervention.

A series of untoward developments between the years 1895 and 1898 determined the course of the United States. Notable was the threat to economic interests in Cuba. In hope of intervention the revolutionaries did their best to disrupt the island's sugar production. They raided cane fields at night, setting them on fire, and when possible burned sugar mills. The Cuban economy was mainly an economy of sugar, almost all of which went to the United States. American companies had invested heavily in plantations and mills. It was perfectly clear that the Spanish government could not protect American property in Cuba. In 1895, Cuban exports to the United States, mostly sugar, amounted to $53 million. In 1896 they dropped to $40 million. In 1897 to $18 million.

Another factor in intervention was the policy of Spain's captain-general in Cuba, Valeriano Weyler y Nicolau, who until his relief just a few months before the Spanish-American War pursued a policy of forcing civilians in large parts of Cuba into so-called reconcentration camps. Tens of thousands of Cubans, perhaps hundreds of thousands, died in the camps, because of Spanish maladministration, dying from starvation or lack of medical care. The Spanish were able to herd the Cubans into the camps and keep them there, but could not handle the camps once they had created them. This extraordinary suffering less than a hundred miles from American shores was almost too much for citizens of the United States. By the end of the year 1897 criticism was so vociferous that the government in Madrid, fearing intervention by the administration of President McKinley, which had entered office in March, 1897, asked the founder and president of the American Red Cross, Clara Barton, to go to Cuba and assist in caring for the *reconcentrados*.

Then came the sinking of the battleship *Maine*, which the president had sent to Havana on a courtesy visit late in January, 1898, after a riot in the Cuban capital appeared to threaten the lives of American citizens. In case of trouble the ship's presence, he believed, might help. Instead, after the ship had spent three uneventful weeks at anchor in the harbor it suddenly blew up. On the evening of February 15, at 9:40 P.M., it went up with a deafening roar. The concussion extinguished all the lights of Havana, and exploding shells from the magazines turned the harbor into a fireworks. A huge cloud of smoke rose up, to the horror of onlookers who in the ensuing quiet could hear the cries of wounded and dying men in the water. The doomed ship went down almost immediately, straight down into the mud, with water rising until only the superstructure was exposed. The toll was 266 out of a complement of 350. Captain Charles D. Sigsbee and anyone whose stateroom or duty allowed him to be on the top deck survived. Men below, asleep in their bunks, drowned like rats.

No one has ever discovered what or who caused the explosion. Surely the Spanish did not do it, for the consequences would obviously have worked against their interests. The revolutionaries, who had conducted the war in the cane fields with sheer abandon, would have had excellent reason to blow up the ship. And yet, over the many years since 1898, not the slightest piece of evidence has appeared that the revolutionaries did the deed. It is a curious situation. If the revolutionaries were responsible, it seems likely some participant would have said something, or some friend or relative would have found himself so full of knowledge that he would have blurted it out. No one should say, in attempted explanation, that Cubans are more talkative than Americans, but someone in Cuba should have talked by now, almost a century after the occasion. Instead there was nothing, and has continued to be nothing, but the fact of the sinking. As one might have expected, two American naval courts of inquiry found in favor of a submarine mine. A Spanish court of inquiry naturally said that an internal cause or causes touched off the magazines. That, incidentally, was entirely possible, for steel warships in the nineteenth century were hardly scientific marvels and it was possible for them to do themselves in, so to speak, through spontaneous combustion in the bunkers or, one suspects, through faulty wiring during the early era of electricity (which had become practical only in 1880). Speaking of the bunkers, it was also possible that some anarchist, maybe in a Pennsylvania coalfield during the strife-torn 1890s, had pitched some dynamite into a coal car, and such an infernal cargo had gotten into the bunkers of the *Maine*. Unfortunately it is no longer possible to examine the ship's hulk, an exercise that in the present day could probably pinpoint the cause of the disaster. After raising the ship some years after the sinking, by putting a cofferdam around it and pumping out the water, the U.S. Navy in 1912 towed it out to sea and sank it in 600 fathoms.

After the *Maine* went down in 1898, war became virtually inevitable. In a Broadway bar a man raised his glass and said solemnly, "Gentlemen, remember the *Maine*." Through the streets of cities and towns, one suspects even down country roads and lanes, went the cry, "Remember the *Maine*! To hell with Spain!"

President McKinley, who was thoroughly aware of the situation, and was no supine politician but a man of intense feeling for the suffering Cubans and for American responsibility, then decided that the United States had put up with enough nonsense in Cuba. He demanded that Spain make peace with the Cubans by October 1, otherwise he would be the "final arbiter" of a settlement. McKinley often has been drawn in the words of young Theodore Roosevelt, who seems to have said about this time that the president had as much backbone as a chocolate eclair. A Chicago newspaper owner saw him in the White House, sitting on a brocade sofa, crying like a boy of thirteen, confessing that he had not slept more than three hours a night, he thought, during the past two weeks. He said that Congress was trying to shove him into war. The latter point was true; the business about the eclair was not. "The major," as he was known from his service in the Civil War, was no fool. He had seen real battlefields and on that score was wiser by a good deal than his assistant secretary of the navy. He wanted an agreement with Spain that would bring peace in Cuba. He knew that the time had arrived for a settlement, one way or another.

McKinley was pushing for Cuban independence. Such a demand, however, proved impossible for the proud government in Madrid, which would only go as far as autonomy. The Spanish government refused the president's terms, and on April 25, 1898, McKinley signed a joint resolution of Congress declaring war.

I

Mobilization

*I*t was an ideal spring day. The American flag was everywhere. As the well-drilled men marched through the streets on that bright spring morning not in holiday attire but clothed in the plain service uniform of the American soldier, their banners flaunting in the air, their bayonets glistening in the sun, surrounded by all the pomp and circumstance of war, with thousands and tens of thousands cheering and waving their kerchiefs, they presented a picture that marks an event not only in local but in national history. By half past four o'clock the last company had reported at Akron and marched to its quarters, and at five o'clock Adjutant General Axline was notified that the entire regiment was assembled with 1,021 officers and men, fully armed and equipped, and awaiting further orders. Every officer reported on Tuesday [April 26, 1898] except two. Lieutenant Colonel Dick, who was in Washington when the call came, reported ready for duty on Wednesday afternoon, and Surgeon Major Farquhar, detained at home by the death and burial of his wife, reported some days later at Camp Bushnell. The Eighth was the first to report its mobilization complete, and it returned a larger number of men than any other regiment in the state.

The rapidity with which the Ohio troops were assembled reflects much credit on the adjutant general's office and on all the organizations. By Tuesday evening, less than twenty-four hours after the call, every regiment in the state, 8,000 officers and men, was at its appointed rendezvous awaiting orders. The Eighth could have left Akron on the twenty-sixth for any point, thoroughly equipped with everything except ammunition and tentage, and no doubt every other regiment in the state was in practically the same condition.

The scenes witnessed by the various organizations on leaving their homes were reenacted at Akron. The people of that bustling, hospitable city abandoned business, pleasure, and everything else and devoted themselves to caring for the soldiers, from the moment of their arrival until the rear end of the last section that carried them to Columbus was out of sight. Many of her leading businessmen today are men who served their country as soldiers in almost every rank during the Civil War. They have the dash and courage and persistency of the practiced and experienced soldier, and, carrying these into their business life, their city has won. The younger men, too, the men of the generation that has come upon the scene of activity since the close of that epoch, display the same energy in affairs and the same public spirit. This was many times demonstrated during the stay of the Eighth in Akron. Early in the evening, after reaching Akron, a number of prominent citizens met at the mayor's office, for the purpose of conferring with the commanding officer, to learn what, if anything, was needed by the regiment, or what could be done to render their stay more agreeable. Among these were the Honorable George W. Crouse, Mayor Young, Captain Aaron Wagoner, Mr. F. M. Atterhalt, Mr. E. A. Hershey, the Honorable L. S. Ebright, Dr. Sisler, Judge Anderson, and Mr. P. E. Werner.[1] We were advised that if we wanted anything all that was necessary was to name it and it was ours. All our needs, however, were well provided for, so that the only thing we could do was to thank them for what they had already done.

Among the courtesies shown us one of the most notable was a dinner to officers tendered by Mr. P. E. Werner on Wednesday evening at his home, at which many prominent citizens of Akron were present. Mr. Werner is of German birth and speaks English with a distinct German accent, but his Americanism is of the most vigorous and lofty type, and would shame some who trace their American ancestry back two or three hundred years. His hospitality was princely and his patriotism intense.

Shortly after midnight Tuesday the commanding officer received a telegraphic order from the adjutant general, directing him to move the regiment to Columbus by the Cleveland, Akron, and Columbus Railroad on Thursday morning at nine o'clock or as soon thereafter as possible.

The citizens of Akron had perfected their plans to hold a public demonstration on the departure of their local organizations—Company B and the band. Now that the entire regiment had become their guests their plans were enlarged to include the whole organization. Colonel P. E. Werner was made chief marshal, business was suspended, shops were closed, and the morning given over to the one matter of seeing the troops start on their journey. A procession was formed on Main Street and escorted the regiment, with Company B, Akron's own company, on the right, to Grace Park where a meeting was held with Mayor Young presiding. Brief addresses were made by Judge Kohler,

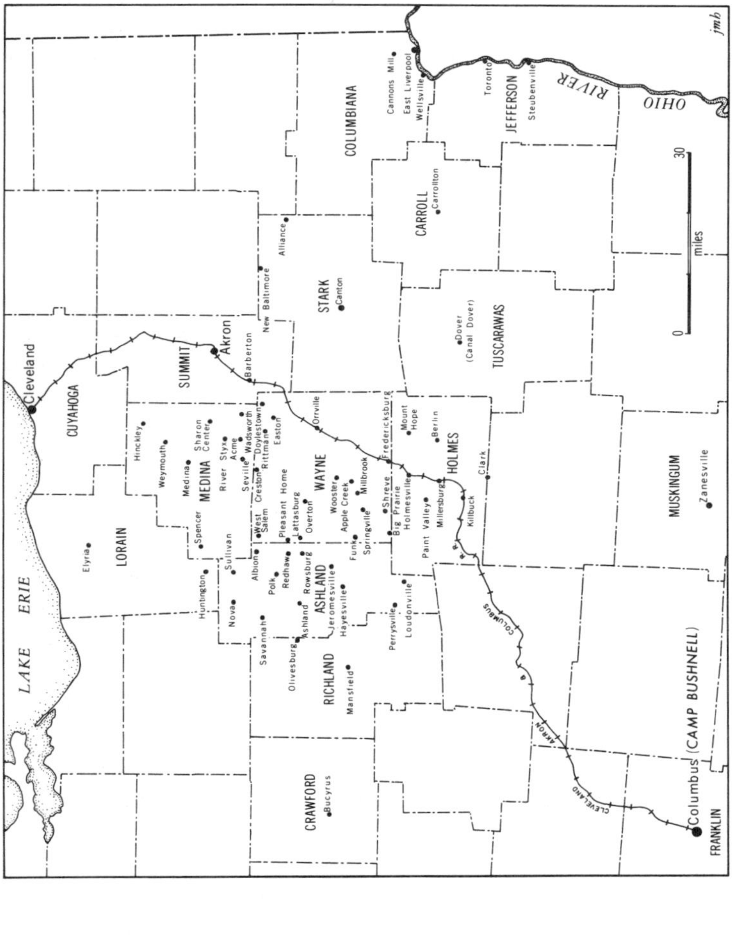

Hometowns of the men of the Eighth Ohio.

Judge Tibballs, the Honorable George W. Crouse, and some of the officers of the regiment.[2] A flag was also presented to Company B. The crowds on the streets were said to be the largest ever seen in that city. Providence seemed again to smile on the undertaking, and the sun shone in a clear and cloudless sky. The exercises in the park were concluded in good season, and the regiment was at the depot ready to embark an hour before the trains were ready. The delay afforded us an opportunity to look at the throngs and visit with our friends. The scene was a striking one. The depot stands in a depression just where the railways pass through a deep cut, with high embankments all around it. North and south of the depot are high and broad overhead bridges, and west of it the embankment gradually ascends to the level of the street and the park which adjoins the railroad. On the level grounds, along the tracks, on all the embankments, on the bridges, on the housetops was a mass of human beings, largely women, wedged in so closely that it was next to impossible to get the soldiers through. It was spring, and every woman seemed to be bedecked in all the brilliancy of spring millinery. As we marched through and mounted the cars we seemed to be a little streak of dull blue, a mere thread, running through a sea of brilliant flowers. If the whole thing had been carefully designed and arranged by a skillful landscape artist its beauty could not have been excelled. It was a charming sight and one not soon to be forgotten by those who witnessed it.

Finally everybody was aboard, the signal was given, and the last section moved off amid the shouts and tears and waving handkerchiefs of 40,000 people. At every station great crowds has assembled, many of them with bands. At Orrville they had a band and a cannon which made as much noise as one of Dewey's thirteen-inch guns. At Millersburg several thousands were gathered with music and cannon, and as each section came in they offered the men coffee, sandwiches, cigars, and other eatables. The only other notable incident en route occurred at Apple Creek where 1,000 citizens of Wooster—whence they had driven across the country some half a dozen miles—awaited the train. During a delay of five minutes Captain J. B. Taylor, A. Saybolt, Jr. and Mr. W. P. Snyder, in behalf of the citizens of Wooster, presented the colonel and chaplain each with a saddle horse and fittings.[3] The commanding officer's horse had been named "General Wooster" by the donors, while that of Chaplain Kieffer had been appropriately christened "Martin Luther." The last section reached Columbus late in the afternoon of the twenty-eighth and it was almost dark when the rear of the regiment marched into camp at the end of a four- or five-mile tramp.

Our experience at Camp Bushnell was such as usually comes with camping and campaigning. Cold and rain, heat and dry, mud and dust followed each other in regular order, and no matter what the character of the weather might be nearly everybody wanted it to be something else. But we at once got down to work and officers and men bent all their energies to fitting themselves for whatever might be before them. Four or five hours each day were given to company, battalion, and regimental drills, in addtion to guard mounting, dress parade, officers' schools, etc. The endless detail of equipment and organization and requisitions and reports made much labor so that everybody was ready to retire when Tattoo sounded.

One cause of much anxiety at this period, with officers and men, was the uncertainty that prevailed as to the number of men that was to constitute the company and the regiment, the character of the formation—that is, whether a regiment was to be composed of ten companies or twelve companies, whether it was to be a two-battalion or three-battalion formation: in short, whether regiments would be mustered into the U.S. service as organized in the state service, or reorganized to conform to the formation then observed in the Regular Army. The National Guard regiments in nearly every state of the Union are organized in conformity with the drill regulations devised by a board of army officers and approved by the War Department and now in use. These regulations provide for the three-battalion formation. While the Regular Army has for a long time recognized the superiority of this formation, and has made its drill regulations on that line, it has never been able to prevail on Congress to authorize it, because, doubtless, of the increased number of officers it would require. Strong pressure was brought to bear therefore to cut down the National Guard regiments to conform to the regular organizations, ten companies, one major, two surgeons, etc. This meant, of course, the disorganization of all National Guard regiments and the dismissal of many officers. On the other hand there was also a strong pressure on the War Department by nearly every state government against any change in the regimental formation of the state troops. The air was filled with rumors about what was going on at Washington with reference to this matter, ninety-nine out of a hundred of which were without foundation. At length, however, it was settled satisfactorily to all the state governments. The National Guard regiments were accepted, practically as organized, one assistant surgeon, the commissary, inspector of rifle practice, hospital corps, and signal corps being eliminated. By this order we lost Assistant Surgeon W. A. Hobbs of East Liverpool, a physician of the highest standing, Lieutenant A. T. Atkinson, commissary of subsistence, Lieutenant A. B. Chapman, signal officer, and Captain A. B. Peckinpaugh, inspector of rifle practice. All of these felt keenly their failure to get in with their regiment. Lieutenant Chapman afterward joined the U.S. Signal Service and spent a year in Cuba, while most of the members of his corps, and of the hospital corps, joined the regiment as privates.

Our hospital corps was also thus wiped out of existence. This seemed to us very unfortunate. Surgeon Smith had an efficient corps of sixteen young men, already enlisted, and eight more ready to join. They were all young men whose tastes led them to prefer that branch of the service, and some of them were medical students. There came a time when we needed them very badly.

Every morning brought forth a crop of new rumors, and every evening showed them to be groundless. The letters written home, and the newspaper correspondence, were filled with predictions as to our destination, the date of our departure was definitely fixed a dozen times a day, and fairy tales were in circulation continually that this regiment was to go to Newport to guard that summer resort, and that one was to be assigned to Washington to act as a "bodyguard" for the President, and another was to proceed to the capital of the nation to guard the Washington Monument. It is somewhat amusing now to go back and read the gossip of the camp as it appeared in the newspapers of the day. A correspondent would write his paper that he had just had an interview with an officer of high rank, who confidentially informed him that his regiment would start for Tampa the next day, whence it would lead the column preparing to invade Cuba. Another advised the readers of his journal, with startling headlines, that Major Blank had just returned from Washington where he had been in conference with the President and the Secretary of War, and had brought back with him an order to prepare his regiment to move at a "moment's notice" to Havana. And so on ad infinitum. These interviews served a double purpose. They supplied the correspondent with material out of which to construct an interesting and harmless letter; and they magnified the consequence of the officer, who thus appeared to an admiring constituency as being taken into the inner counsels of the Republic in this great emergency.

It was while we lay at Camp Bushnell that we received news of Dewey's great victory at Manila. This was so stupendous as at first reported that everybody thought the "intelligent contraband" of Civil War days had been resuscitated and was getting in some more of his war stories. But when it was confirmed the men in that camp were thrilled with joy, and at the same time just a little bit afraid the whole fabric of Spanish colonial government would collapse before we could get ready to take a hand in pulling it down. The enlisted men were put through their physical examination on the tenth and eleventh of May, and the officers on the twelfth. The officers all passed but two—Captain Marquis of Company M and Lieutenant Blackburn of Company B. The examining surgeon pronounced both of these officers subjects of heart trouble that would unfit them for active service. When they came back to the regiment, after having heard their fate from Major Howard, which was that they could not be mustered in, their dejection was pitiable. They went directly to their quarters and remained there, and a little later when an officer was sent to bring them to headquarters for the purpose of devising some scheme to secure a reversal of the surgeon's decree they were found almost in tears. After some maneuvering and much pressure a way was found to overcome the objections of the surgeon and both were next day mustered with the rest of the regiment. Both went through the service and both were quite sick but not from heart trouble—unless the little affair which afterward culminated in a wedding to which Lieutenant Blackburn was a party may be called heart trouble.

Soon after our arrival at Camp Bushnell, Major Vollrath was assigned to duty on the staff of General Axline as an assistant adjutant general and served in that capacity during our stay in that camp. Captain F. C. Gerlach of Company D was appointed by Colonel Coit, commander of the Second Brigade, assistant inspector general, and Lieutenant W. O. Rutherford of Company B was at the same time assigned to duty on the staff as an aide-de-camp, both serving until the brigade was disorganized by the departure of the regiments for other camps.

On the thirteenth of May we were mustered into the service of the United States for two years, as the Eighth Ohio Volunteer Infantry, by Captain C. M. Rockefeller. Lieutenant Colonel Dick who had found it necessary to return to Washington on the twenty-ninth of April in connection with his duties as secretary of the Republican National Committee reached camp in time for the muster, as did also Major Farquhar who had been detained at home by the death of his wife. We were thus enabled to muster the full complement, 889 officers and men.[4]

Captain Rockefeller, the mustering officer, afterward met a sad fate. He was assigned to duty in the Philippines early in 1899. He reported to his regiment on April 28. On the twenty-ninth he went out alone to examine the picket lines and no trace of him has ever since been found. It is supposed he went beyond the lines by mistake, was shot by the Filipinos, and his body destroyed or left where it never will be discovered.

Simultaneously with the muster in of the regiments came an order assigning them to the different camps of construction, established principally in the South. The First Cavalry and six regiments of infantry were sent to Chickamauga, Fernandina, and Tampa. The Seventh and Eighth Regiments and the 9th Battalion—colored—were assigned to Camp Alger near Washington. As soon as this was definitely known Captain Kuhns, the quartermaster, was sent forward to Alger to lay out the regimental camp and arrange for the necessary transportation to meet us at the end of our railroad journey and transfer the tents, baggage, etc. He left on Monday morning the sixteenth, meeting at Pittsburgh Lieutenant Colonel Dick, who had left for Akron on the fifteenth, and going thence to Washington. Captain H. O. Feederle was appointed acting quartermaster during the absence of Captain Kuhns, and Lieutenant Philip Yost of Company I was detailed as regimental commissary. Lieutenant George M. Wright, adjutant of the 2nd Battalion, was appointed ordnance officer a few days earlier and he promptly discovered that he had on his hands a contract of magnificent proportions. Major Bryan, who was in command on that day in the absence of the colonel, at once complied with the order, and transportation was arranged for nine o'clock, Wednesday, May 18, over the Chesapeake and Ohio Railroad.

Shortly after our arrival at Camp Bushnell the friends of Colonel Dick and Adjutant Maynes at Akron, and of Captain Kuhns at Canton, presented each of them with a fine saddle horse. Captain Maynes' mount, a fine little black, was taken sick and suddenly died four or five days before we left Bushnell. Mr. W. H. Mullins of Salem, a friend of the adjutant, learning of the situation, wired him an offer of a very fine mare for his use which the adjutant accepted. He thus had the distinction of riding the finest and most valuable mount in the service.[5]

The seventeenth was spent in completing arrangements for our movement to Washington. Many friends of the regiment came in that evening or early the next morning to bid their acquaintances good-by and see them break camp.

II

Washington

The regiment traveled in three sections. The first in charge of Major Vollrath carried the 1st Battalion; the second under Major Bryan carried the 2nd Battalion; and the third with Major Weybrecht in command carried the 3rd Battalion, the band, and headquarters. A surgeon and hospital steward accompanied each section. At every town or hamlet through which we passed there were crowds of people with bands and flags; and at one or two stations we observed large gatherings with baskets, evidently filled with good things. It came out that these were intended for the Seventh Ohio which had companies from that section of the state, and which was to follow us in an hour or two.

The last section of our train left Columbus just about twelve o'clock noon. We crossed the Ohio River at Point Pleasant about dark. At Charleston, West Virginia, although it was ten or eleven o'clock at night there were many thousands congregated, among whom were of course many colored people who furnished the boys much amusement.

At Charlottesville, next day, we stopped for coffee and sandwiches. There were many old Confederate soldiers among the crowds and they were the most enthusiastic patriots in the lot. After leaving Staunton somebody discovered two colored boys only twelve or fourteen years old, who had secreted themselves under one of the coaches and were hanging on to the iron rods. In this position they rode to the next stopping place, some forty miles. They were here taken on board by some of the officers who employed them as servants. One of them was left at Camp Alger sick; the other accompanied the regiment to Cuba and back.

We reached Dunn Loring at half past four the afternoon of the nineteenth. Here we were met by Captain Kuhns with transportation for our tentage and other impedimenta and were soon on the march to Camp Alger, two and a

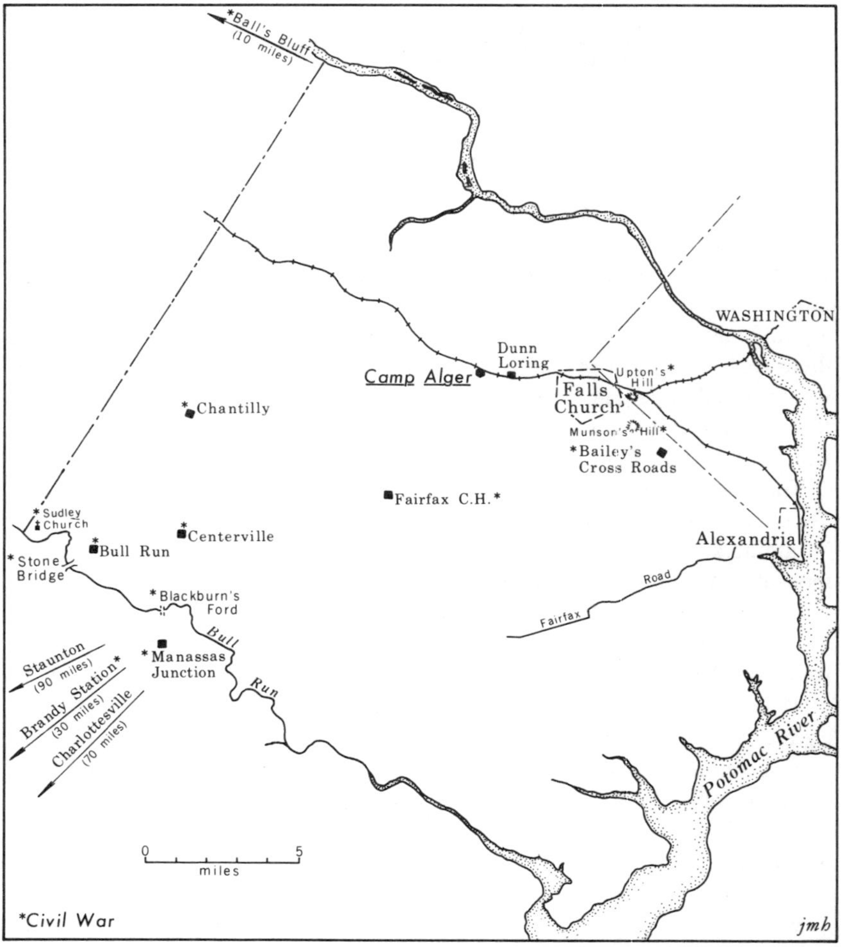

Camp Alger in Virginia, where the Eighth Ohio encamped before assignment to Cuba.

half miles distant, over a fairly good but somewhat dusty road. It was nearly six o'clock when we turned into Camp Alger, and threatening rain. Only two or three regiments appeared to have preceded us—the First D.C. and a couple of Pennsylvania regiments. Lieutenant Colonel Dick and Captain Kuhns had selected a very desirable location for our camp, there being as yet no officer on the ground in command, and the quartermaster had laid it out as nearly according to regulations as the configuration of the ground would permit.[1]

The wagons with the tentage followed closely, were unloaded in a twinkling, and in less than twenty minutes after we halted the tents were up, the men all assigned, and the preparation of supper begun. Then, as if in continuation of our Camp Bushnell experience, it rained for nearly an hour. It was warm, however, and no unpleasantness marked our first night in the third stage of our journey, Camp Alger.

Camp Russell A. Alger, at which we were destined to pass nearly two months of our time, was located about nine miles west of Washington, in Virginia, two miles and a half from Falls Church, and the same distance from Dunn Loring. A steam railway from Alexandria passes through both of these stations, and an electric line runs from Washington to Falls Church. Communication between the railway, at both of these points, and the camp was maintained by means of all sorts of vehicles known as "fixes," drawn by all sorts of horses and driven by all sorts of people from the typical "coon" to the ordinary intelligent farmer, and all bent on turnng an honest penny out of the necessities of the situation. If the mortgages on the properties in that portion of Virginia were not all removed during the summer of 1898, it was not because the natives failed to work their gold mine.

The spot on which the II Corps pitched its tents is historic ground. It is part of the territory originally surveyed by Washington. In this immediate vicinity thirty-seven years before, nearly 500,000 American soldiers were gathered, out of whom were organized on one side the famous Army of the Potomac, and on the other the equally well-known Army of Northern Virginia. The very spot on which the Eighth's tents were set and over which we tramped a hundred times daily was once the scene of a running fight between Mosby's men and a body of Union cavalry. A few miles to the north is the scene of General Baker's fight and sad death at Ball's Bluff. Just east of us were Munson's Hill and Upton's Hill which the rebels fortified with Quaker guns and which became the starting point for McDowell's army on its fateful march to Bull Run in July 1861. Twenty miles west is that famous battlefield twice the scene of bitter defeat to our arms. Over these roads and through these fields and villages swarmed a mob of defeated and demoralized Union soldiers, followed at a safe distance by another mob of Virginians and South Carolinians almost as badly scared and disorganized. Chantilly, Brandy Station, Centerville, Fairfax Court House, Manassas Junction, Bailey's Cross Roads, Blackburn's Ford, the Stone Bridge, and Sudley Church are all close at hand; and an hour's ride by steam would carry one to the Blue Ridge, beyond which lies the beautiful Shenandoah, with Harpers Ferry, Winchester, Cedar Creek, Tom's Brook, the Opequan, Strasburg, Berryville, Staunton, and a hundred other hamlets made famous by Sheridan's campaigns up and down the valley. In the summer of 1898 there was assembled on these same hills an army of Americans animated by a common purpose, inspired by a common patriotism, and equipped with all the destructive enginery of war to be later employed against a common enemy. Men of Massachusetts and Virginia, Ohio and Tennessee, Pennsylvania and Carolina, Illinois and Missouri, were now, side by side, cultivating the arts of war on the field where a few years before their shafts had been leveled at each other. The corps was commanded by General Graham, a veteran soldier of the Union Army. The First Division, of which the Eighth was a part, was under the command of General Butler, a one-legged Carolina Confederate; and more than one group of the more elderly officers was gathered after Retreat, in which under the inspiration of a "Gato" and a sip of "Hunter" for the stomach's sake were recalled vivid recollections of scenes in which some of them had played parts on opposite sides of the stage. If the war with Spain accomplished nothing else, the obliteration of sectional differences is ample compensation for all the outlay.[2]

The new regiments came pouring into camp two or three a day. For a time there was more or less confusion, but by the twenty-fifth order was pretty well established. The First District of Columbia, whose camp adjoined ours, left on the twenty-first for Chickamauga. During the two days and nights we had been neighbors quite a warm friendship had grown up between the two regiments. The men were intelligent, gentlemanly, and well-drilled and disciplined; and the officers knew their business. They made a fine appearance as they marched out. We were destined to meet them again under less favorable circumstances, and we found them again the same high-toned soldiers. They were escorted out of camp and halfway to Dunn Loring by the 1st Battalion of the Eighth under command of Major Vollrath. The Sixth Illinois arrived on the twentieth and went into camp on the east side of the narrow road that ran through the grounds, directly opposite the Eighth. The Sixth Massachusetts marched in about noon, Sunday the twenty-second, escorted, as had been the Illinois boys, by the band of the Eighth, and were conducted to the ground just vacated by the District of Columbia. The three regiments thus brought into close relationship by mere accident were a few days afterward made the Second Brigade, First Division. Colonel D. J. Foster of the Sixth Illinois became commander of the brigade by reason of seniority, his commission bearing date of May 11, while those of Colonel Woodward and the colonel of the Eighth were dated on the thirteenth. The two latter a few days afterward drew for rank, and Colonel Woodward got second place. The Sixth Massachusetts were a fine-looking lot of men, well-drilled, and the best-equipped regiment that came into the camp. The men from Illinois had the unmistakable Western swing and easy air about them, noticeable even to Ohioans, who are not themselves exactly Easterners; but they were robust, well-behaved, and when they lined up for duty a soldierly lot of fellows. Colonel Foster continued in command of the brigade until June 8 when General George A. Garretson reported and took command. The assignment of General Garretson to our brigade was highly gratifying to everybody, especially so to those of us who knew him personally. He was a soldier by training and experience, and at the same time he had spent the greater part of his life in active business pursuits in the city of Cleveland, so that he was neither a martinet nor a mere "political" general. He was coolheaded and imperturbable, and impressed those about him as one of those fellows who don't lose their heads or their nerve—as the boys put it, "don't get rattled." Much of our good luck in receiving equipment and supplies was due to the quiet, businesslike manner in which he went after what was needed without any parade or advertisement of what he was going to do or had done. When by one of the accidents of the campaign we became separated it was a cause of great regret on the part of the Eighth, and there is a good reason to believe that the separation caused him quite as great disappointment.[3]

One of the first things the general did was to call on the commanding officer of the Eighth for an aide-de-camp on his staff. Lieutenant George M. Wright was at once recommended and appointed and he served to the close of the war with the highest ability.

When we first went into Alger there were half a dozen board shanties on the north side of the Fairfax Road, such as you see on the borders of a country fair, in which were offered for sale everything the owners could think of likely to tempt the appetites of the soldiers. The number of these delicatessen palaces rapidly multiplied as the population of the camp increased, and the boys promptly named the aggregation "Shantyville." Around these mushroom, tawdry "Metropolitan Restaurants" and "Delmonico Hotels" they would congregate like flies around a molasses barrel, particularly after night when they were ablaze with the glory of gasoline lamps, and exchange their good money for vile circus lemonade, green apple pies, black cigars, and unripe bananas, after which they would wind up the banquet with a dish of ice cream containing all the elements of that toothsome delicacy except cream. About midnight the trouble would begin, and from that time until the coming of the morn in russet mantle clad, all the surgeons and hospital stewards and hospital corps men in the camp would be busy getting the kinks and knots out of the intestines of a hospital full of men who couldn't imagine what had made them sick. Next day the yellow papers would have a sensational exposition of the spread of sickness caused by the bad water.

There was much discussion in the press as to the healthfulness of Camp Alger, and after we left it was abandoned as result of this agitation. Unfavorable conditions may have developed after our departure but while we were there it was altogether a very desirable ground. The well from which we drew our supply of water was equal to all demands and the water was excellent. The soil was porous, and the surface rolling, so that after a rain it soon dried off. In the interest of truth it must be admitted that we had a very liberal supply of dust, but that is only uncomfortable, not destructive of health. We had some sickness here, the result of a change to camp life and camp diet, but as a whole the physical condition was excellent. We had our hospital tents up and well-organized, and nearly every regiment that came in to camp dropped some of its sick or exhausted men there for temporary treatment. The first death in the camp was that of a Sixth Illinois man who came in very sick and died the next day. Chaplain Kieffer with a detail and the band of the Eighth attended the funeral and conducted the services. The first death in the Eighth was that of Private Fred G. Haushalter of Company B, which occurred on the twenty-eighth of May. He had been slightly ill only a day or two and nobody thought him in a serious condition. Just before Taps, when Surgeon Farquhar, Captain Maynes, Captain Feederle, and the commanding officer called at the hospital tent the indications were that he would be about in a day or two. In an hour, however, he grew rapidly worse and a little after midnight he died. In the morning his company escorted the remains to Falls Church where Chaplain Kieffer held brief services in the open air and the body was forwarded to his home at Akron, accompanied by a guard detailed from his own company.

Death did not again visit us for nearly a month and then it came without warning and selected as its prey the most widely known and best beloved character in the regiment, Chaplain I. N. Kieffer, who died in his tent on the morning of June 23. Chaplain Kieffer at the time of his death was serving his country for the second time as a soldier. He was a private in the 120th Ohio Infantry, and a noncommissioned officer in the 169th Ohio, during the Civil War. When the call came to the Eighth to assemble he promptly reported for duty. He then said that he had only one favor to ask and that was that if the regiment was anywhere in the United States he wanted a leave of absence to return home in June at the time of the commencement of the University of Wooster. The promise was made, and he was at home for a week. Returning he reached camp on the eighteenth. Up to the time of his leave of absence he had been in excellent health, thriving upon the open air life and the fare of a soldier. When he rejoined us he looked worn and sick, a condition which he and we attributed to his much visiting and his long journey. For four or five days he continued in this condition, never taking to his cot save for brief periods, and at times feeling almost well. Neither he nor the surgeon nor those about him thought anything more serious than a disturbed digestion was troubling him. But about half past three o'clock on the morning of the twenty-third his life left him in a flash, in the twinkling of an eye. Hospital Steward Oppenheimer, who was in his tent with him and Surgeon Wuchter who was in the adjoining tent, heard him utter a little cry, jumped instantly to his assistance—there was a gasp for breath, and it was over.

The body was placed in front of his tent, the military services held in the presence of the entire regiment under the charge of Dr. J. G. Butler of Washington, for whom he had engaged to preach on the next Sunday, and then the remains were taken to Dunn Loring, escorted by Company D, Captain F. C. Gerlach, and six captains acting as pallbearers—Captains Kuhns, Feederle, Marquis, Charlton, Willis, and Hill—whence they were forwarded to Wooster. At Wooster his death created great excitement and overwhelming sorrow. The war was already beginning to claim its victims. His funeral on Sunday was said to have been the largest ever held in that city.

Shortly after reaching Camp Alger an order was issued by Lieutenant Colonel Girard, the corps surgeon, directing the surgeon of each regiment to make a careful inspection of his command to determine how many of them needed vaccination. Surgeon Wuchter inspected the Eighth by companies and found a large percentage needed it. The men were marched to the surgeon's quarters with the left arm bare to the shoulder. One of the surgeons did the cutting, and Hospital Stewards McKinney and Oppenheimer applied the points. The operation was performed with neatness and dispatch. Occasionally some sensitive fellow at sight of the blood on his arm would swoon and have to be carried off. In a week or ten days half the men were walking about with sore arms, but no serious results followed.

Then every officer and man was supplied with a "first aid" package. This is a packet about the size of a pocket cigar case containing antiseptic compresses, bandages, and other appliances to be used in case of wounds. Each day the officers' school and the noncommissioned officers' school were instructed by Surgeons Smith and Wuchter in the methods of rendering first aid to sick and wounded men, arresting hemorrhages, applying the dressings contained in the package, and in the duties of litter bearers in carrying off wounded. This seemed to some of the timid very much like leaving a measure for a coffin, and it impressed everybody with the understanding that the situation was daily becoming more realistic.

On the twenty-fourth of May the Eighth was called on for a company to encamp at Dunn Loring for the purpose of guarding the commissary and quartermaster stores at that point. Captain Marquis of Company M with his company was designated for that purpose. This was a desirable assignment as it gave the captain an independent command with all the opportunities for demonstrating his personality that attach to such a position. A few days later a second company was called for and Captain Lee with Company G was sent to report to Captain Marquis. The officers and men of this detachment aquitted themselves creditably, and on being relieved two weeks later to return to the regiment the depot quartermaster paid them a very high compliment for their efficiency.

The excellent discipline and conduct of the men of the Eighth, their soldierly bearing, and the observance of many of the little amenities that pass between gentlemen at once attracted the attention not only of the other troops but of the authorities and the general public. Their bearing up to the last moment justified the good opinion entertained and everywhere expressed regarding them. Without ostentation, and with strict truthfulness, it can be said that no regiment in Camp Alger excited as much interest, received as much commendation, entertained as many visitors, and made as many friends as the Eighth. It was a little thing, for instance, for Sergeant Palmer, the leader of the band, to double-quick down the road with his band when he saw the Sixth Illinois coming, and play them into camp. It cost nothing; but like all civility it touched a tender chord.[4]

On the twenty-fifth of May the President issued a call for 75,000 additional volunteers. The first call for 125,000 was about filled, but the organization into larger units was not yet perfected and their equipment was not complete. The War Department therefore consumed several days in concluding its regulations for enrolling men under the new call. The most important conclusion reached was that one which provided that new recruits were to be added to organizations already in the service.

The enlistment of recruits was simply a matter of selection. At nearly every point there were many more applicants than could be accepted. It was therefore a short task. The first squad of the "rookies," as they were called, to arrive was a lot of twelve men from Akron for Company B who came trudging into camp on the morning of the thirteenth. They were greeted good-naturedly with cries of "fresh fish," and cheers. They looked odd in their "derby" and "fedora" hats, with their little bundles containing their wardrobes in their hands, covered with Virginia dust, and evidently amazed at the signs of a great encampment of soldiers about them. They were soon made welcome, however, and forgot their embarrassment.

From this time on the squads came in daily, until by the twentieth all had reported. They were clothed and armed as fast as they arrived so that in a few hours they could only be distinguished from the old men by their awkwardness. They were on the whole a desirable lot of men and made good soldiers. Some of them at first had peculiar ideas about subordination. One young gentleman was detailed to chop wood or bring water for the company cook and flatly refused. As one of the newspaper correspondents put it, "he was jerked to the guardhouse so quickly that he did not have time to reconsider. The next morning the court told him he might chop wood for five days." The same young gentleman at a later period of his military career refused again to do some duty to which he was detailed, and he got a dose of medicine that cured him. Just before he was mustered out he talked bravely of his purpose to assail some of his officers, but he never hurt anybody.

For the next fifteen days the recruits were put through their paces by the sergeants in squad drill, and by their officers in company and battalion movements, guard duties, etc., at a lively rate.[5] They learned quickly and could not be distinguished from the old men in drill. They lacked the seasoning, however, which time only can give, and it was destined to tell on them.

Although the daily routine consumed most every moment of time from Reveille to Retreat there was yet opportunity for relaxation and recreation. And the two or three hours between Retreat and Taps, which are the exclusive property of the soldier not on duty, gave an opportunity for indulgence in all kinds of sports and entertainment. Two or three evenings each week the band gave concerts as near the center of the camp as possible, always attracting large audiences not only from our own but from neighboring commands. There were frequent "spreads" or "banquets" during an evening, based on a box from home. There were improvised bands making night hideous with their discords, and there was often good singing in some of the company streets. Once there was a dress parade of the "rookies" which was really a work of art.[6]

Among the characters who at length became a part of the situation was one whom everybody in Camp Alger saw and heard—the Irish newsboy. He was about fifty years old as men reckon time, but he had had a hundred years of fun. He was surrounded by a sort of a "he may have seen better days" atmosphere. He had a maroon nose; and there were traces on his features leading up to the suspicion that under strong temptation he might be beguiled into looking upon the wine when it is red. When he cried his wares in Fairfax County he could be heard at Hampton Roads. But in his profession he was a genius. He came into camp loaded with his papers, like Atlas with the world on his back, just as rosy fingered morn was painting the eastern sky. He usually got there before Reveille did. As he came over the brow of the hill and struck headquarters street, he burst forth like a clap of thunder from a cloudless sky, "Here's yer *Post!* Gitcher *Washington Post!* Latest from the front! Gitcher *Post!* 'Nother great victory! The Boys in Blue! They licked the Dons again! Gitcher morning *Post!* Morro Castle bombarded! Old Glory floats o'er the ramparts! Gitcher *Post!* The yellow-skinned Dagoes in full retreat! The Gem of the Antilles will soon be ours! Gitcher *Washington Post!* Great consternation on the Atlantic coast! Cervera's fleet sails proudly up the St. Lawrence! Git a *Post!*" And so on without end. There was neither cessation nor break in his harangue until the last paper was sold; then he vanished into thin air and was seen and heard no more until daybreak the next morning.

III

Getting Ready

As the time approached when our departure for some point nearer the seat of activity became more certain the desire to join the Eighth increased. We could have organized two more full companies right in Camp Alger without effort. There were daily applications from numbers of men, some with and some without credentials, who wanted to get into our regiment. Among the appplicants were two nephews of President McKinley, James F. McKinley and John D. Barker, who came to headquarters on the twenty-third and presented the following letter:

Executive Mansion
Washington, June 23, 1898

Dear Colonel Hard:

This will be handed to you by my nephew, James F. McKinley, who has lived in Canton with my mother and our family for many years, indeed ever since he was a little boy. He wants to enlist. He prefers to go with your regiment, and in this determination he has my approval. I hope you can find room for him, preferably in Company I. He is a good boy. I am very fond of him and have the deepest interest in him. He is only 18 years old, possibly rather young for a soldier, still I can but admire his patriotism and so send him to your regiment for enlistment. I hope he will make a good soldier.

I cannot forbear to congratulate you personally upon the good things I hear about your regiment and yourself, and you have my best wishes for its success and yours.

Sincerely yours,
William McKinley

Colonel C. V. Hard
Eighth Ohio Volunteer Infantry

The president was of course at once advised that the young men would be enlisted in Company I as he had requested. They were examined, mustered in by Major Bryan, and given a furlough until next day to carry their civilian effects back to Washington, and walked into the White House full-fledged soldiers.[1]

A day or two later another young man of about eighteen or twenty, Charles Philips of New York City, came to headquarters with a letter from the president asking that he be allowed to join the regiment and if possible the same company as his two nephews. He was at once mustered in, and assigned to Company I. He made a good soldier, was always ready for duty, never lost his nerve, and particularly gained the esteem of his comrades by his devotion to the sick. He retained his health until the journey home on the *Mohawk* when the seed of malaria in his system developed. When we landed at Montauk his mother was waiting outside the guard line to meet him. The meeting was an affecting scene. She scarcely recognized the yellow, emaciated, bearded youth before her. A furlough was at once granted him and the sad yet happy mother took him home with her. He barely recovered in time to be present at the muster out of the regiment ten weeks later.

Another young man who joined the regiment just before we left for Santiago was Ralph Burton. Burton had been in camp ever since its formation as a correspondent. He had made every effort to have his papers give him an assignment with some of the troops going to the front. Failing in this, on the day of our departure he sought a place in the ranks, which was given him. He hustled around and got himself uniformed and equipped, and when we fell in for Dunn Loring he was in line ready for duty. Burton made a good soldier, but he was stricken with the fever and came very near finishing his earthly career and leaving his bones at the camp at Shafter's headquarters.[2]

The quartermaster of a regiment has charge of the property of the command, the tentage, the transport, and the supplies generally. The clothing and some parts of the equipment of the men are drawn and issued by him. In case the regiment moves it is his duty to arrange transportation by rail or water, subject of course to his superior officers in the same department.

The subsistence of the men devolves upon the commissary, and the issuing of arms, ammunition, etc. is the duty of the ordnance officer.

The quartermaster of a regiment is a regularly appointed officer of the staff and in the present organization ranks as captain. The commissary and ordnance officers are detailed from among the line officers, a lieutenant usually, and are exempt from other duties while serving in these capacities. Regulations provide however that the quartermaster may act as commissary if necessary for any reason. The commissary's position is not a very desirable one in some respects. If the supply of subsistence is for any reason unsatisfactory—if it is short, or defective in quality or in variety, or if one company gets all the good meat, and another thinks it gets all the bad—the commissary must bear the blame. At Camp Bushnell and at Alger, for a short time Lieutenant Yost acted as commissary. He begged to be relieved and was sent back. Then Lieutenant Hard was appointed, and after a brief experience he expressed a strong desire to return to his company. One or two other lieutenants were detailed, but after a brief service in each case they intimated that their ambition in that direction had been fully gratified. At length Captain Kuhns in sheer desperation agreed to undertake the unpleasant task.[3]

At Camp Bushnell, Lieutenant G. M. Wright was appointed ordnance officer, and in a short time had matters in his department thoroughly systematized. On his appointment as aide on the staff of General Garretson, Lieutenant C. F. Schaber was detailed to succeed him. Lieutenant Schaber took up the work where he found it and carried it through with the highest degree of efficiency. By the time we were ready to move these departments of the administration were thoroughly organized.

Shortly after General Graham took command of II Corps the commanding officer inquired of him if there would be any objections to taking the Eighth Regiment for a practice march of two or three days. General Graham approved of the plan and authorized a detail to be sent out to the Potomac to examine the route. A few days later, however, an order was issued from corps headquarters detailing a plan for having the whole corps undertake practice marches by regiments and brigades. Under this arrangement the Eighth set out for the Potomac on the morning of the twenty-seventh of June. The distance was about ten miles. We reached the ground selected shortly after noon, pitched tents, posted guards, had dinner and then everybody was given permission to bathe in the river, a privilege of which all availed themselves. The next morning after an early breakfast we struck tents and marched back. General Garretson had planned for a sham fight, on the march back. The Sixth Massachusetts preceded us an hour or such a matter, and were to lay in wait for the other two regiments—the Sixth Illinois and Eighth Ohio—at some point on the road. Major Weybrecht with the 3rd Battalion had the advance, and the column was preceded by a strong line of skirmishers covering a front of nearly a mile. A short distance north of Dunn Loring the skirmishers met the outposts of the Massachusetts men and the firing began. The Eighth Ohio and Sixth Illinois were at once deployed to the front, moved up through woods and fields until they found the Massachusetts line, and then the roar of musketry for half an hour was deafening. The affair ended when the ammunition was exhausted. A few men were burned with powder, the defenses were captured, and the whole brigade marched into Camp Alger tired and dirty and hungry.

The degree of excellence and efficiency in any military body depends of course in large measure upon the intelligence, patriotism, and spirit of both the officers and men. In the matter of patriotism there was nothing lacking in the volunteers. Animated by the highest motives they had taken up arms of their own volition. Add to this in the Eighth a high degree of intelligence in the men, and of character and efficiency among the officers, and the distinction gained by the regiment at this time is properly accounted for. Frequent demands were made on the Eighth for capable officers to perform special duties, and the drafts were never dishonored. Immediately after assuming command of II Corps, General Graham appointed Major Vollrath of the 1st Battalion on his staff as provost marshal of the corps. In maintaining order in a camp just organizing with men who were, most of them, wholly unaccustomed to the restraints of military discipline, and at first indisposed to submit to them, and with a cloud of fakirs surrounding the grounds and trying to invade them with their shoddy wares, and their insanity-producing whiskey, he had on his hands a contract of magnificent proportions. No disturbance, however, occurred that was not promptly quelled, and vendors of moonshine and other death-dealing viands soon learned the advisability of viewing Camp Alger from some Pisgah height several miles away. *En passant,* that "moonshine" whiskey was a decoction that must have been compounded by the Alchemist of Hades. If a fellow got a good drink of the vile mixture inside his system, in ten minutes he became a raving maniac. A number of instances occurred where men under the influence of this intoxicant became unmanageable, and were tied and dragged to the center of the parade ground, a quarter of a mile from everybody, where they were allowed to yell and kick to their heart's content. Only a few cases occurred in the Eighth Regiment, and no man who had dallied with the seductive potation once was ever stirred with an insatiable ambition to wrestle with it a second time.

Lieutenant G. M. Wright, the first ordnance officer of the regiment, in equipping the command came into frequent contact with the ordnance office in the War Department and with headquarters of II Corps. His knowledge of all the details of the equipment, the accuracy with which his reports were rendered, soon attracted attention. Only a few days after General Graham appeared upon the scene, he discovered Lieutenant Wright and ordered him to report at corps headquarters where his efficiency could be utilized for the benefit of the whole corps.

We had civil and mechanical engineers of first-class ability for almost any emergency. When the practice march to the Potomac was first contemplated, the commanding officer inquired for a civil engineer to take charge of a detachment of men to go over the territory, select the best route, determine upon a camping ground, locate springs or other water supplies both upon the road and at the destination, and make an accurate map of the country and the roads. Lieutenant E. E. Brosius of Company K was designated for that duty and allowed to select his own detachment. He found a number of noncommissioned officers and privates who had had considerable experience in that direction, and with them went over the line, traveling about fourteen miles going down to the river in the afternoon of one day, and ten miles coming back the next morning. After he had returned and completed his map, the corps commander having determined to order all the regiments in the corps to make the same march, Lieutenant Brosius was summoned before General Garretson and then before General Butler, commander of the division, where his maps were examined and his description of the country received. That map thereafter served as a guide for all the troops making the march to the river.

At another time, early in the encampment at Alger, Major Weybrecht when acting as field officer of the day, determined to have an accurate map of the country, showing the locations of the exterior guard, the outposts, and the regimental camps. He directed Sergeant Major Brown of his battalion to go over the country, make an accurate estimate of the distances, and execute such a map. This was done, and the map drawn was afterward passed along from each field officer to his successor and served as the guide and authority in establishing the outposts.

Lieutenant Yost of Company I, who is a civil engineer, was also ordered to corps headquarters where he served for several weeks on General Graham's staff in engineering work. Later he performed some excellent work of this character in Santiago.

Then there was Lieutenant K. W. Taylor of Company C, who had a specialty of his own. If there arose in the daily discussions of officers or men any question concerning drill regulations, military etiquette, army regulations, constitutional law, affairs of state, history, or even theology, requiring settlement, the lieutenant was called in; and he could generally refer to the paragraph, page and volume of some authority that would decide it. His readiness in these matters gave him the nickname of Old Authority.

Among our officers we had at least six lawyers. These were Lieutenant Colonel Dick, Major Vollrath, Major Bryan, Captain Lee, Captain Hill, and Captain Marquis. There were a number of lawyers and students of law among the men. We could have supplied the corps with judge advocates.

Two of the captains were pharmacists—Captains Gerlach and Fisher. When the fever struck us and we had more sick men than we could well care for, their knowledge enabled them not only to look after the health of their own companies, but to render great assistance to the overworked surgeons in ministering to the wants of the others. Lieutenant Birk of Company A had left his class at medical college, just about to graduate, to join his company. He also in the time of distress came to the aid of the sick on Sevilla Hill and at Santiago. There were bookkeepers, teachers, manufacturers, builders, merchants, and men of almost every branch of business among the officers. The field, staff and line, taken altogether, was a body of gentlemen of the highest order of zeal, activity, and efficiency.

The enlisted men of the regiment, the men "behind the guns," the men who after all make up the great whole known as an army, were just as interesting. When corps headquarters wanted a stenographer and typewriter from the Eighth the names of four were sent up—and they took them all. If any special work was to be done at any time—telegraphing, telephone repairs, building, surveying, writing, bridgebuilding, blacksmithing, or mule driving—we had the men right in our ranks who could do it. At one time many of the horses belonging to the staff and to the New York cavalry troop were taken sick. At once an order came down to the Eighth to detail one veterinary surgeon with directions to report immediately at headquarters. They had heard of Sergeant Bowman who was a very skillful veterinary surgeon. When we were in Cuba, after the surrender, Sergeant Bowman was ordered by cable to go from Santiago to one of the camps in Florida to take charge of a large body of sick cavalry horses.

Another man in the ranks, Private Brown of Company D, frequently took charge of the Christian Endeavor meetings held in a large tent at Camp Alger, and on one occasion went down to Washington and addressed a large meeting in one of the public halls, held in the interest of some patriotic commission, at which the Secretary of War, General O. O. Howard, and other men of national repute were speakers.[4] There were among our men many students from college, students of law, and medicine and dentistry and even theology. So that we had soldiers capable of doing everything from preaching to mule driving, and several, by the way, who thought they knew better how to command a regiment of infantry than the colonel did.[5]

The story of life at Alger would be less than half told if it failed to record at least an allusion to the social side of experience in that camp. The large number of Ohio people residing in Washington and those visiting the city, of course, were interested in the soldiers from their own state. Scarcely a day passed that did not afford us the real pleasure of entertaining from one to a dozen or more at dinner or supper, at headquarters mess, and every company in the regiment had its guests at more or less frequent intervals. The camp of the Eighth was geographically so placed that everybody going into Camp Alger struck our quarters first, and, indeed, went through our streets from necessity.[6]

One of the most interesting and suggestive visits we had was that from a number of surviving members of the Eighth Ohio of the Civil War. The officers of the Eighth spent a pleasant hour with these survivors of the older Eighth with two of whom, Captain Griswold and Captain Johnson, the commanding officer of the later Eighth had been acquainted at the time of their service in 1861.[7]

The heroic, somewhat dramatic, but wholly unsuccessful attempt to close the entrance to Santiago Bay, by sinking the collier *Merrimac* in the narrow channel, was made by Lieutenant Hobson early on the morning of June 3. Just a week later, June 10, a detachment of some six hundred marines was landed at Guantánamo Bay forty-odd miles east of Santiago, gaining a foothold, known as Camp McCalla, which was held only after a number of days of severe fighting and considerable loss of life.

On the fourteenth of June, V Corps, numbering approximately 17,000 men, sailed from Tampa, Florida, under the command of Major General Shafter, charged with the invasion of Cuba. Eight days later, June 22, the disembarkation took place at Daiquiri, a few miles east of Siboney. There was little or no resistance, and no loss of life.

The first passage at arms occurred on the twenty-fifth of June. Lawton's division was ordered to occupy a position three miles west of Siboney, Bates was to support Lawton, and Wheeler was to guard the rear between Daiquiri and Siboney. During the night of the twenty-third, Wheeler, with a semi-brigade under General Young, pushed 'way ahead of Lawton, and in the morning ran up against the Spaniards at Las Guásimas. In ordinary wars this act would have cost General Wheeler his sword. But this war was different. After a fight of an hour or two the Spaniards were driven back. Our losses were 16 killed and 52 wounded out of 964 men engaged—about seven percent. Compared with Gettysburg, or Chickamauga, or Spotsylvania, it was not a large affair. There were many skirmishes in the Civil War with greater losses, that were disposed of in a report of half a dozen lines and were afterward never heard of. But Las Guásimas demonstrated the dash, the eagerness, the persistency and the endurance of the Americans. From that moment the Spaniards had a wonderful respect for the American soldier. The next séance led them to hold our boys in awe and veneration.

This rapidly moving procession of events excited the liveliest interest in Camp Alger. The air was charged with speculation, and gossip and rumor, as a thunder cloud with electricity. Ninety-eight percent of the gossip with reference to our probable movements was based wholly on imagination. The other two percent had a foundation. Once the Philippines were said to be our destination. There was just a little talk at one time about sending Garretson's brigade to that portion of the globe. We were really assigned to sail for Cuba on the twenty-second of June. The reason for the selection of our regiment and brigade at this time, to be attached to Shafter's army, was simply that the reports and inspections which reached the War Department showed that we were the best-equipped, best-drilled, and best-disciplined body of men in the camp, and therefore best "fit" for service.

But for reasons not divulged in the orders, the order directing our brigade to embark for Cuba was revoked, and the 33rd and 34th Michigan sent instead to constitute a brigade with the Ninth Massachusetts under General Duffield. Their equipment was so deficient that we were robbed to supply them. They left Alger on the twenty-second, and we "lagged superfluous on the stage," disappointed, crestfallen, and mad.

It was after this miscarriage that we made the ten-mile march to the Potomac and return—June 27—to which reference has already been made. It was quite apparent that we were slated to move if additional troops were required in Cuba or elsewhere. The progress of events in Santiago seemed to indicate a need of more men in that province, and we stood on the edge of expectation continually.

Things were now happening in rapid succession. On the morning of July 1 the attack on El Caney by Lawton's division, and on Santiago by Kent and Sumner, began. Before noon of that day it was known in Alger that a fight was in progress. Next day the information received indicated heavy losses and some degree of success. The third was "blue Sunday" sure enough. Shafter was palpably rattled and seriously contemplated abandoning the position his men had taken at such cost and withdrawing five miles to a strong line east of San Juan River. His dispatch to the War Department intimating this purpose caused the cold shivers to run all over that stately pile of granite, whence they shot across the street and made the very windows in the White House rattle. This sudden change in the situation and the request for reinforcements was interpreted as an admission that our army had run up against something that caused it to stop and scratch its head and think. At midnight, however, the Secretary of War cabled Pecos William [Shafter] to hang on and that reinforcements were coming. At the same time orders were sent to Garretson's brigade to be ready to embark at an hour's notice for Newport News to take transports for Cuba. The orders reached us on the fourth, the anniversary of the great Declaration. Then a little later, the *St. Paul* having gone to New York to take on supplies for Shafter's army, the Eighth Ohio was directed to go to New York by rail and board that steamer in time to sail Wednesday morning, July 6. The order occasioned some excitement and much satisfaction, and everybody set to work packing and putting on the finishing touches. We were to take the cars at Dunn Loring at two o'clock on the fifth. We did not do it. On the contrary it was midnight when the first section left that animated entrepôt. As is most always the case in such matters, there first came up one and then another impediment to delay the movement.

Tents were struck about noon; the wagons assigned to us for transporting baggage to the railroad were loaded and started on their journey; the officers' horses, saddled and bridled, were brought out; the ladies in the camp, wives of the officers who had remained, determined to stay until the last moment, sat around on empty boxes in the glaring sun, waiting to say the last good-by; the bugler stood at headquarters ready to sound the Assembly; the men sat around on the ground or on their rolls smoking, talking and ready to "fall in" at the signal. Then came an orderly with verbal information that the train would not be ready for us until five o'clock.

While we loitered around, waiting till the shadows were a little longer grown, surrounded by the debris of our abandoned camp, Major George W. Baird, paymaster U.S. Army, drove in with a little iron box and a little dapper clerk, and announced his purpose to pay us off. There is no well-authenticated case recorded in history of a thoroughly disciplined soldier refusing to accept money tendered to him, and the boys of the Eighth marched fearlessly up to the paymaster's improvised quarters and boldly accepted their little fifteen sixty per.[8] It tells volumes of their thoughtfulness and good judgment that eighty percent of this money was at once converted into checks and sent home in the evening mail to fathers or mothers or wives.

At length an orderly rode up with the information that our train would be ready in an hour. The officers' wives, save two or three who had resolved to postpone the parting to the wharf at New York, said good-by and started for Washington whence they were to take the cars for Ohio; there were a few gulps of emotion in spite of an assumed air of joviality; the bugles sounded Attention; the men promptly fell in and the march to Dunn Loring commenced.

It was dark when we got there. Quartermaster Kuhns had provided a supply of hot, strong coffee which was distributed to the men on our arrival. Then we sat around on the ground, in the midst of Cimmerian darkness, and waited five hours until our train was ready. It was after midnight when the first section pulled out and we bade farewell to "Old Virginny."

IV

Aboard the *St. Paul*

The first section of the train, carrying the 1st Battalion, reached Jersey City about half past seven o'clock Wednesday morning July 6. We were greeted here by a number of our friends and an army of news reporters.

The second section with the 2nd Battalion arrived some two hours later, and the 3rd Battalion came in an hour behind the second. The 1st Battalion, with which were the commanding officer and most of the staff, were marched on board the ferryboat *John F. Darcy* a half an hour after their arrival and transported to the foot of Courtlandt Street, New York City. We at once marched to the wharf of the American Line of steamers, only a few blocks distant, where the *St. Paul* was lying taking on supplies.

The coming of a body of soldiers, hastening to take a transport for Cuba, had doubtless been heralded. When the gates at the ferry were thrown back and the head of the column emerged into the broad landing place, it encountered a crush of human beings. The crowds were patriotic, and enthusiastic, and demonstrative. They blocked the way in front so that the squad of fifteen or twenty policemen, detailed to maintain order, with difficulty cleared a way for the head of the regiment, and they pressed on the flanks, seizing the men by their hands, patting them on the shoulders, and even throwing their arms around them as they marched along. They seemed to be in a frenzy of patriotism. All along the line, from one wharf to the other, there was an unbroken cheer, while the air was filled, as with the rattle of musketry, with such ejaculations as "Good boys!," "God bless you!," "Bully for Ohio!," "You can always bet on the Buckeye State!," "Boys! We're proud of you!" It was an ovation that would have caused the blood to tingle in the veins of the bronze statue of General Jackson.

Great city as it is, it had so happened that very few of the troops, on their way to the camps, or to the front, had, up to that time, passed through New York.

At Washington, near which city a corps of 25,000 or 30,000 men was encamped, soldiers were so numerous on the streets and about the hotels that they had long ceased to attract attention. But in New York, on this day, if one of the Eighth boys appeared on the streets anywhere he at once became the objective of a friendly mob, and a corporal's squad of them could have blocked the traffic on Broadway in two minutes. An amusing instance of this affectionate curiosity occurred during the forenoon. When we were paid at Camp Alger the day before there was an amount of something more than eight dollars due each of the original enlisted men for which it had been necessary to make a separate roll. Because of the lack of time before we began the march to Dunn Loring, Major Baird was unable to pay this portion to the men, and at his own suggestion he gave the commanding officer a check for the total amount, some $8,000, on which the money could be drawn in New York as we passed through and distributed at leisure en route to Cuba. About eleven o'clock, accompanied by Mr. D. M. MacLellan of New York, a friend of Adjutant Maynes, who had volunteered to furnish the proper introduction at his bank, and a guard of two men with rifles, the commanding officer went to the Chatham National Bank on Broadway, for the purpose of getting the cash for the paymaster's warrant. The guards were left standing at the door while the business was being transacted inside, without any suspicion that they would attract any notice. But in less than two minutes a crowd of a thousand persons had gathered around the corner looking at the soldiers on the doorsteps and peering through the windows at those inside. The cashier, looking up from his desk, where we were engaged in making some calculations, was alarmed at the dimensions of the crowd. Fearing the impression would get abroad that there was a run on the bank, he called for the police, who came and forced the crowd to move on. The soldiers were then called inside the bank, and the business was concluded, the officers putting themselves to much inconvenience to supply the money in the various denominations required.

If any Eighth Ohio man made a move to purchase any commodity, liquid or solid, some citizen was sure to step up and insist on his right to pay the score. One of the boys, walking along the street and drinking in the novel sights, was accosted by a gentleman who said to him, "Do you belong to this Ohio regiment that is going to Cuba?"

"Yes, sir."

"Well, I can't go myself, but I'm proud of you boys who are going, and I want to do something for you. Take this!" And he handed the young soldier a new crisp banknote with a figure 10 on it.

The dock at which the *St. Paul* was lying, taking on stores and waiting for us to embark, was an immense two-storied affair, eight hundred feet long and nearly two hundred wide. The battalions as they arrived were marched upstairs to the second floor, which was cleared for our accommodation. Guards were placed at the entrance and strict orders issued that nobody should be allowed to pass without permission from headquarters. The information at that time received by the commanding officer was that as soon as the remaining companies of the regiment arrived, the *St. Paul* would be ready to take us on board and move out, and as they were liable to reach us at any moment it was necessary to confine the men to the building to keep them from getting scattered and left behind. Later in the day, when it became evident that we would not sail before evening, a good many passes were issued to men who were reliable, for short periods.

Immediately after reaching the dock the commanding officer went on board the *St. Paul* to pay his compliments to Captain Sigsbee, and to get information as to when he would be ready to have us embark, how the men were to be assigned to quarters, and what arrangements were made for subsisting the officers and supplying the men with coffee. He imparted the information that his executive officer, Lieutenant Driggs, had arranged with the steward to furnish coffee to the men, and to subsist the officers at a reasonable rate, with the officers of the steamer, and suggested that an officer of the regiment be designated to adjust that matter with Lieutenant Driggs at once. At the same time he extended an invitation to the commanding officer and the lieutenant colonel to accept the hospitality of the captain's mess. The invitation was accepted, and during the voyage these two officers were enabled to enjoy many hours of delightful and instructive conversation in Captain Sigsbee's cabin.[1]

A large majority of the men of the Eighth had never been in New York, and the temptation to get out and see the sights, even if they were obliged to violate orders to do so, was almost irresistible. As they looked up the cross streets leading toward Broadway, and saw the streams of humanity surging backward and forward, and heard the din and roar of traffic, it was almost more than the best-disciplined soldier could stand to remain cooped up in that enclosure on the water front. And it was more than some of them did stand, as was soon demonstrated.

The schemes devised for securing passes were multitudinous, and they were as brilliant as they were numerous. It was astounding, the number of men who found it necessary to go out and get a toothbrush, or a comb, or a piece of soap. There were some who wanted to go to a telegraph office to wire their friends at home. That proposition was worked until a number had been directed to a Western Union station right on the wharf, and inside the guard lines, when that was abandoned for something more plausible. One young man had a sister living only a few blocks away, who was too ill to come down to the wharf, and he must go and see her before he sailed away. Another wanted to get some medicine of a particular kind, adapted to his peculiar ailment; and so on ad infinitum. The sick relative racket was successfully worked a number of times.

Suddenly, however, the demand for passes began to decline, and at length wholly ceased. There seemed to be no further desire on the part of anybody to see the city. The guards at the head of the stairway became conscious of the fact that their occupation was like that of the celebrated Mr. Othello—it was "gone." By a curious concatenation of circumstances it was noticed just about this time that the number of men in the dock seemed to be very much diminished, and that groups of men in blue could be seen everywhere on the street going in every direction. The fact is, the boys had gotten ahead of the authorities, and had discovered a way to get out into the city and see their sick relatives, and buy their toothbrushes and combs, without being subjected to the humiliation of asking for passes. And this is how they did it.

There were a number of trap doors in the floor of the second story, or upper deck, of the wharf, which shut down flush with the floor. From these doors iron ladders led down to the first floor. The scheme was like the electric telegraph or the steam engine—easy enough when you know how. It didn't require an immortal genius to work it out. Forty or fifty men gathered around one of these trap doors, the door was quietly raised, and thirty of the forty quietly "glode" down that ladder and out to freedom. The crowd concealed the open door and the exit of the men, and if an officer approached the door was closed, a few rolls and haversacks and guns dropped on it, and by the time the officer reached the circle everybody was busily engaged in discussing the latest news from Manila or the likelihood of our reaching Santiago before the surrender.

About noon a representative of the great tobacco house of Lorillard and Company came on to the wharf and requested permission to present the men with a quantity of tobacco. The permission was, of course, promptly granted before he had time to change his mind. In a short time there came down a wagon bringing a great supply of Climax Plug, enough to give every man in the regiment a pocketful, which was put on board with our other subsistence. There came a time when that tobacco was reckoned worth its weight in gold. It was landed with our rations at Siboney. When that hamlet became the yellow fever camp for all Santiago, and intercourse with it was interdicted, the boys organized a squad, and walked the nine miles to Siboney and carried the tobacco out to the regiment. They marched through rain and mud and jungle, in the hot sun, through booming rivers, right into a yellow fever nest, and left thirty days' rations untouched, but got that tobacco because, as they said, they "needed it in their business." They would have charged a masked battery for one "chaw."

During the day it seemed that nearly every Ohioan in the city called to bid us Godspeed. Many prominent people, other than these, also visited us. All of them expressed regret that the regiment had not marched through the city, and urged us strongly to do so yet. Yielding to these frequent and urgent requests it was at length determined to take a short tramp as it then appeared that there would be an abundance of time; this would employ the men, would keep them together, would enable them to see something of the city and to stretch out their legs before going on shipboard to be cooped up in narrow quarters for four or five days and nights. Our friend Mr. MacLellan again came to the rescue, and rushed off to secure the necessary permission from the city authorities. He returned about three o'clock, the officials having arranged to clear Broadway from 34th Street down. Captain Sigsbee on being consulted as to the probable time of sailing replied that he would leave at five o'clock, and all who were not on board then would get left.[2] This of course made it impossible to make the march. It was sincerely regretted by everybody, as we were all vain enough to imagine that we could show New York 1,300 pretty good-looking Buckeye soldiers.

About four o'clock General Guy V. Henry and General Adelbert Ames appeared on the scene. General Henry had been assigned to the command of a division consisting of Garretson's brigade—the Eighth Ohio, Sixth Illinois and Sixth Massachusetts—and Duffield's brigade then in Cuba. He at once notified the commanding officer, verbally, of the fact that we were under his command. General Ames was ordered to report to Shafter at Santiago for assignment. Congressman Wadsworth of New York also came aboard just before we sailed and accompanied the expedition.[3]

At length, however, the labor of loading the baggage and stores and ammunition was ended. The wheezy derricks ceased their grating and squeaking. The quartermaster's detail came up from below fuming and sweating and swearing—just a little. The clear shrill notes of the Assembly shot out from Jimmie's bugle, and went bounding back and forth from one end to the other of the great wharf, and were picked up by other buglers and hurled out of the front windows into the streets below. There was the sharp command of the captains and the hurry and scurry of the formation. There was an endless procession of men marching down the long gangplank, the dull thud of the rifle butts on the sounding floor, and the rattle and clatter of coffee cups and steel bayonet scabbards. There was the impatient ejaculation of some officers, "Hurry up there, sergeant! What in———are those men so slow about?," and the final good-by with the fellow who happened to have a friend among the throngs admitted to the pier. There was the continuous fusilade of witty gibes and jeers aimed by those on board at the others coming down the gangplank.

There was the usual rivalry for place in the assignment of quarters, and all the attendant controversy—when there is only one "best place" and twelve companies want it there are sure to be eleven companies making life a burden for some poor officer, and there was the friendly scramble for desirable points from which might be seen the receding lights of the city as we dropped down the bay. Then came the cry from the executive officer, "Is everybody aboard?," and the answer from the pier, "Everybody's aboard!," and the little group of officers who had remained on the wharf to see that the last straggler was sent down walked over the bridge onto the steamer, the planks were hauled in, the hawsers loosened, the last telegram, a message from Governor Bushnell bidding the Eighth Regiment Godspeed, was drawn up by a line in a little water bucket after all connection with the dock had been severed, the great engines were set in motion, the ship quivered a little, the band struck up the "Star Spangled Banner," everybody uncovered, and at half past seven o'clock the *St. Paul* glided out into the river, amid the shouts of the thousands on the wharves and housetops, with 1,325 men of Ohio bound for Santiago and they knew not what. Only one man was left; the 1,326th, although seen an hour before, did not appear, and was never with the command again. This story does not record his name.

We passed at close quarters a steamer loaded to the guards with excursionists who cheered and waved their hats and handkerchiefs, while our band greeted them with patriotic airs, and the boys cheered and waved their campaign hats.

The sun was just going down as we steamed out. The thousands of lights, from the streets to the crowns of the highest buildings in New York and Brooklyn and Jersey City, the lights and many-colored signals on the vessels in motion or lying at anchor, the penetrating rays of "Liberty Enlightening the World," all made a picture that will probably never be effaced from the memory of these who looked upon it that night.

At just ten o'clock we passed Sandy Hook Light. The *St. Paul* turned her nose a little more to the southward, and we were afloat on the high sea, sure enough bound for Cuba.

The *St. Paul* is a vessel of the American Line of transatlantic steamers, built in an American shipyard, by American workmen, of American steel, under an agreement with the government that in case of war the Navy Department may take possession of her and convert her into an auxiliary cruiser. Her dimensions are magnificent. Her length is 554 feet, breadth 63 feet, depth 42 feet, and her measurement nearly 12,000 tons. An idea of the strides made in navigation since the discovery of the New World may be derived from contrasting this leviathan of the deep with the little 80- and 100-ton caravels in which Columbus sailed away in his voyage across the unknown sea.

The appointments of the *St. Paul* are princely in keeping with her magnificent proportions, and she is provided with every convenience that human ingenuity can devise. At the time of the war she had been partially dismantled in her transformation to an auxiliary cruiser. Her armament consisted of eighteen pieces: six 5-inch rapid-fire guns, six 6-pound Nordenfeldts, and six 3-pound Hotchkiss guns. She was commanded by Captain Charles D. Sigsbee, whose connection with the tragic end of the *Maine* in Havana harbor, only a few months before, had made him an historic character.

The vessel carried a crew, including a detachment of marines, of about 450 men. These, with the 1,325 men of the Eighth, the extra passengers, and a body of some 50 stevedores, made a human cargo of nearly 2,000 souls. In addition to this she carried a large quantity of clothing, ammunition, entrenching tools, subsistence, etc. for Shafter's army, and thirty days' rations for the Eighth.[4]

This heavy load caused her to set deep in the water, and she rode the sea like a monarch.

The voyage, up to the last moment, was delightful. The sea was smooth, the sky clear, and no storms were encountered. There was very little sickness. It had been generally understood that when we passed Cape Hatteras we would, of course, run into stormy weather. But we sighted the Hatteras lights about eight o'clock on Thursday evening while the sea was almost as calm as Odell's lake. The first night out many of the men slept on the decks and found it agreeable. The second night the rain drove them onto the lower decks and into the holds. After that, however, as many as could find a place to lie on sought the decks. Because of the crowded condition of the vessel it was impossible to observe any regular military exercises or ceremonies. The adjutant did devise a sort of a dress parade, which we went through every evening. It consisted in the color guard, at the sound of the Assembly, marching with the colors into the forecastle, the band playing the "Star Spangled Banner," and the officers and men informally gathering around uncovered. At the conclusion of the music, Retreat was sounded and the assemblage dispersed. It was simple, and only a small portion of the regiment could participate in it, but it served to keep us in remembrance of the fact that we were soldiers and not pleasure seekers.[5]

On Friday or Saturday, as we were nearing our destination, an inspection by companies in heavy marching order was directed to be held, for the purpose of putting everything in proper condition for the landing and participation in the assault on Santiago, which it was assumed would take place as soon as the reinforcements of which we were a part had reached the coast. There was much speculation, all around, as to just how everybody would conduct himself in the fighting which appeared to be before us, and a quiet determination, without any bluster or bravado, to do nothing to discredit ourselves or our friends.

Soldiers and sailors fraternized with each other at once. In a very short time the landlubbers reckoned the time by "bells," talked about "knots" instead of "miles," spoke of the "leeward" and "windward" sides with marvelous familiarity, and indeed knew all the technical jargon of the sea. The "Jackies" were very friendly and accommodating and sold the boys all the coffee they wanted at five cents a cup. When we landed we found it was our own coffee they had sold us. Those sailors were a very demure and childlike aggregation, but they had the true commercial instinct. Saturday morning about ten o'clock we passed San Salvador Island within two or three miles. Columbus must have been suffering from an acute attack of nostalgia when he landed on that sterile reef. It is said that when he touched terra firma he fell on his knees and gave thanks to God that his lines had fallen to him in such pleasant places. Then he sat down and dictated to his typewriter a letter to Ferdinand and Isabella in which he told an enchanting tale of scenes marvelously beautiful and picturesque, of trees of luxurious foliage, of flowers of gorgeous hue, of roses that burdened the air with their redolence, of delectable fruits growing wild and in endless profusion, of the rapturous songs of the birds clothed in gay plumage, of the pure and balmy atmosphere, and the cool and limpid waters that burst from numberless springs in the hillsides. That description of San Salvador, based upon imagination, and contravened by facts, is enough to make the Chief Prevaricator of the *New York Journal* retire into some sequestered dale, far from the madding crowd, and despise himself.[6]

Nearly every piece of real estate the Spaniards got hold of in the New World they named after some saint, and dedicated to the Church; then they proceeded deliberately and systematically to rob the men of their golden trinkets and despoil the women of their honor. Columbus named the island on which he landed San Salvador; the irreverent English dubbed it Cat Island—plain, common, everyday Cat. This historic reef is some fifty miles in length, and from five to eight miles in width. It lies low and seems to have some green on its surface, and much more white. From the decks of the *St. Paul,* with the most powerful glasses, no sign of a human habitation could be seen save the lighthouse and its adjacent structures. It is said that three or four hundred people eke out a miserable existence by raising sheep and eating fish. The inhabitants wear as little apparel as they did when the *Pinta* first hove in sight and paralyzed them with fear in 1492—which was none at all. Occasionally some civilized sailor is forced to land there by stress of weather, or to leave something to eat for the lightkeeper, but when he pushes his little skiff away from the shore and says good-by, he raises his voice in paeans of thanksgiving quite as lofty as those sung by Columbus when he landed. In fine San Salvador in a barren coral formation worth nothing save as a piece of bric-á-brac. We must not be too hard on Christopher, however. Ferdinand and Isabella had staked him for the play of his life and he wanted to show them that they were getting their money's worth.

The last night of the journey Captain Sigsbee used additional precautions against attack. We were approaching the Windward Passage through which we would sail before morning, and it was possible some stray Spaniard might run across our path. He therefore directed that no lights should be burned in the ship, and that everything should be kept absolutely dark. Orders were also issued to the soldiers that in case of an alarm in the night, those sleeping on the decks were to be aroused and hustled into the hold out of the way and as much as possible out of danger. Everybody lay down that night with the idea on his mind that he might be routed out before morning.

About midnight the alarm came. It was dark as Egypt, and utterly quiet save for the rumble of the engines. Suddenly the word came down from the lookout that a suspicious-looking craft was approaching, and in an instant almost could be heard the command of the sergeants from one end of the ship to the other, "Everybody below!," "Everybody in the hold!," "Everybody down!" For a moment or two there was a shuffling of feet and a rattling of accouterments, with an occasional growl or Sunday School speech from some half-awake soldier, then the decks were cleared, the guns loaded, their crews stood by awaiting further orders, and everything was as quiet as it had been before. Within ten or fifteen minutes the vessel was discovered to be a United States cruiser, the men came back on deck, and nobody was hurt—just scared a little.

V

Cuba

We passed Cape Maisí about daylight, turned westward and went skirting along the south coast of Cuba. Everybody was astir as soon as the sun rose, and drinking in the scenery on the island. Everywhere could be seen U.S. vessels of some character—men-of-war, transports, hospital boats, dispatch boats or something. We sailed right into the midst of a fleet off the entrance to Santiago Harbor, where Captain Sigsbee reported to Commodore Schley on the *Brooklyn*, and received instructions to take us back to Siboney some fifteen miles for disembarkation. We had a fine opportunity to see all of these historic vessels at close quarters, and we could also see the wrecks of the Spanish fleet strewn along the coast.

We were within gunshot of Morro Castle, and with our glasses could readily distinguish the flag floating over it, and the men moving around. They doubtless could see that the new arrival was a troopship with a large body of men, as our soldiers swarmed on the decks and in the rigging like bees.[1]

Returning to Siboney, one hundred rounds of ammunition and three days' rations were issued to the men and preparations made to disembark at once. Two officers of General Shafter's staff came off to us immediately after we hove in sight—Lieutenant Colonel John J. Astor and Major S. W. Groesbeck. They brought orders to General Henry to land with the troops as rapidly as possible, and conduct them to the front. After lunching with us these officers returned to the shore.[2]

The troops were landed in regular order, Major Vollrath's battalion being the first. They were rowed ashore about three-quarters of a mile or sometimes a mile in rowboats holding each about eighteen men beside the sailors, and landed on the beach. The sea was quite rough, which made the work of getting the men with their kits down into the boats, and then rowing them ashore, difficult and somewhat dangerous. It was all accomplished, however, without serious accident, and by six o'clock the last man of the battalion was safely dumped out on the beach. Night was rapidly approaching, the sea was still heavy, and the sailors pretty well worn out, and Captain Sigsbee refused to allow them to work longer, so that we only succeeded in getting one third of the regiment ashore on that day. This was a disappointment to us, as we could hear occasional artillery firing in the direction of Santiago, and were told that there had been some sharp infantry fighting. Major Vollrath marched his battalion out about three-quarters of a mile or a mile from the landing and encamped for the night on a plantation, and around the ruins of a house, the property and home of General García, the celebrated Cuban patriot.[3] At five thirty the next morning the work of disembarking was resumed, Major Bryan's battalion being the first and Major Weybrecht's the last. It was a slow and tiresome operation, and made some of us who were on shore waiting for the end of it almost wild with impatience and nervousness. General Henry, too, who was waiting to go out with us, became very restless. Yet nothing could be done to expedite the landing, as every boat and every sailor was employed. At length the last man jumped ashore, the regiment was formed, and we started over the bottom road, as it is called, for Santiago.[4]

Siboney from the decks of the *St. Paul* was rather an inviting picture. The harbor is not a harbor; it is simply a place where you can get down to the water without jumping off the cliffs or being let down by a derrick. It is a slight depression or recession in the straight line of the coast with a small level territory a few hundred feet in width on which the hamlet stands. A diminutive mountain stream empties here into the Caribbean Sea, a stream that may be as dry as a powder horn at two o'clock, and at two thirty a raging torrent. On either side the sea comes right up to the mountains, and the coast is a perpendicular face of stone apparently as smooth and regular as if it were the handiwork of human architects. From the decks of the transport it looked as if the mountains had been broken in two and pulled apart a little way to let the stream through, and the earth leveled down at the gap. All around it—east, north, and west—was a background of mountains clothed in luxuriant green such as only the climate of Cuba can produce.

The white or light blue huts of the natives under the glaring rays of a noonday sun looked clean and inviting, and the groves of tall palm trees with their broad-leaved tufts at the top were a tropical vision to men who had just come from the land of oaks and elms. Here and there, high up the mountain-sides, or on the very top, was a blockhouse, built by the Spaniards with great skill, and abandoned with greater agility when the Americans went after them. Groups of tents occupied by quartermaster and commissary details, the hospitals, and the one or two battalions of infantry guarding the base of supplies, were pitched on every available spot: on level ground in or near the village, or hanging on the mountainsides where they looked as if they would fall off if they were not tied. Squads of American soldiers, easily distinguishable by their uniforms, and other squads of Cubans in their white trousers and jackets and broad-brimmed sombreros, were seen moving around and giving life to the scene. Altogether it was a beautiful panorama.

That was the way the picture looked from the steamship a mile out at sea. But when we got ashore over the rickety little pier, or waded up onto the beach through the surf knee-deep or neck-deep according to the mood of the waves, it was—well! It was different!

Those white huts were filthy comfortless hovels such as civilized men would hardly house their dumb animals in. They were evidently designed to keep out the rain and sun and to keep in the filth and poisonous air of the occupants. When we passed them we held our noses. The ground on which we halted to await the coming of the balance of the regiment had been occupied a few days before by a portion of García's army, and was littered with camp refuse and decayed and decaying fruits that made the air positively nauseous. The ground was everywhere, save right in and around the quarters of the Americans, covered with filth, and all the surroundings indicated a state only a little advanced beyond barbarism. The white trousers and jackets of the Cubans on closer view were found to be of white cotton, never washed, dirty, and with the "grease of ages" on them. They—the Cubans, not the white trousers—waded out into the surf waist-deep, seized great strips of fat bacon on the lighters, carried it on their bare heads up the beach and threw it on a great pile where other Cubans in their bare legs and bare feet tramped over it and corded it away. Of course this bacon was intended for the relief of the Cubans, and if they were content with this method of handling it, it was not for us to protest.[5]

The Cuban soldier as he made his debut at Siboney was not an imposing spectacle. Clad in the scant and motley habiliment of his race, bare, often, as to his feet, armed with every variety of rifle known to modern warfare, with the ubiquitous machete hanging by his side and a haversack of woven straw on his back, without drill, or discipline, or cohesion or organization, coming when it was his pleasure, and going when he desired, and always hungry, his mien was not designed to inspire the loftiest admiration. And when they circulate among our troops, selling them green and overripe fruits, and fruits not intended to be eaten by human beings, at twenty times their worth, defrauding and speculating off the men who had left their happy homes to liberate them, they seemed to some of us more like banditti or freebooters than patriots struggling for that freedom that is the just aspiration of the highest type of manhood. We may, however, temper with charity our judgment of these dusky and shoeless warriors. Our ancestors traced their way with blood from bare feet in the snow at Valley Forge, and endured hardness as good soldiers for eight long years without pay and on mighty scant fare, and they gained their independence. Perhaps the end of the Cuban suffering will be a prosperous republic on this sunlit and fertile island. Or destiny may lead it to become a part of the greatest republic the world has ever seen, and whatever the outcome history will say of us that we helped to do it.

About half past one o'clock the last man was ashore and the regiment was at once formed for the march. Captain Kuhns with a detail of fifty men was left to unload the baggage and the thirty days' field subsistence which was to be our sole reliance for a time at least.[6] General Henry with his staff all mounted and guided by an officer of General Shafter's staff led the way out of the village and to the trail which we were directed to follow. The officers of the Eighth were all on foot, our mounts having been sent by another transport. Just before we marched out Colonel John F. Weston, corps commissary, now commissary general of the army, very kindly offered the commanding officer one of his horses for the march to Santiago on condition that his return was guaranteed that night. The offer was accepted, and his use was divided between the field and staff officers at the head of the column. Private John S. Rhorer of Company K was detailed to ride the horse back to Siboney after we had gone into camp that night. He did it and faithfully delivered the horse to his owner, but he had an experience in the storm and darkness that he will always remember. The march of nine miles was over what was called the bottom road, between two ranges of mountains most of the way, and the heat was stifling. We met many parties of liberated *reconcentrados* from the interior, hurrying to Siboney to get something to eat—always something to eat. There were also numerous other parties encamped along the trail. At one place in a shack constructed by setting up poles with forked ends on which was supported a roof or covering of branches and leaves with the sides and one end enclosed by the same material, we counted seventeen or eighteen men, women and children living on the bare ground—principally women and children. Once while the band was playing for the purpose of enlivening the boys a little, we met a large group of these *reconcentrados*, who danced and sang and waved their bandannas like a delegation escaped from a lunatic asylum. What seemed to us commonplace and matter of fact was to these unsophisticated and simple-minded people as entrancing as the music the morning stars are supposed to have sung together about the time of Creation. We halted once to get our wind at the brow of the hill on which the Battle of Las

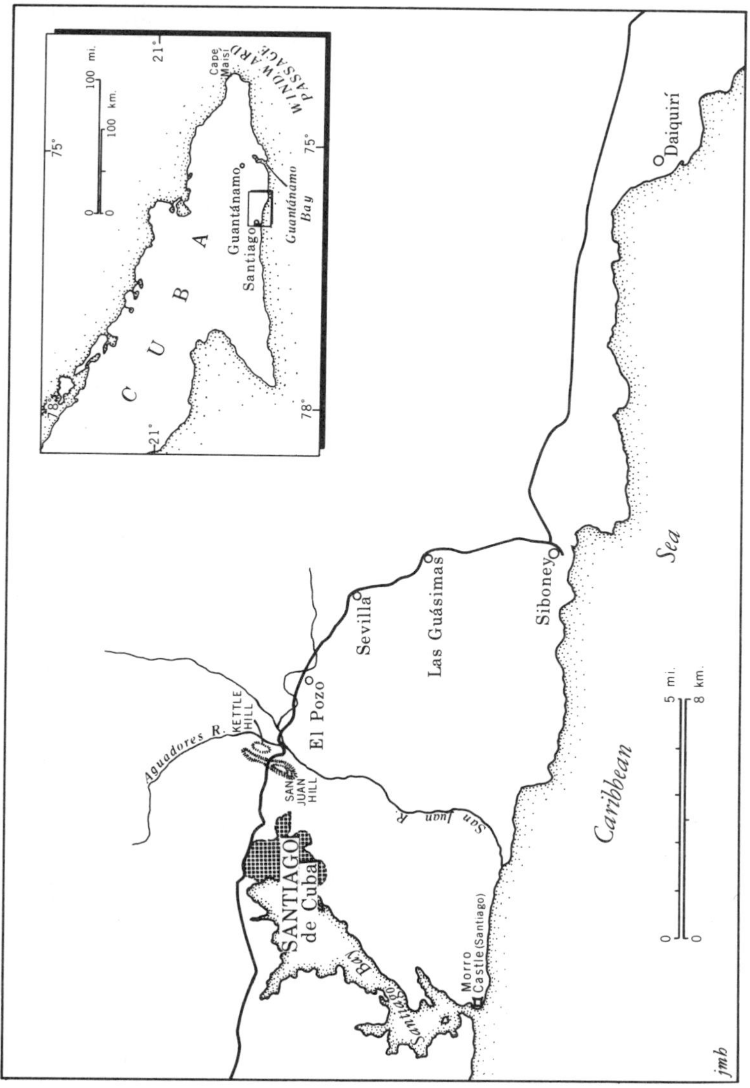

Area in southern Cuba where the Eighth Ohio was stationed.

Guásimas was fought. Just where the head of the column rested, near what appeared to be the very old ruins of a building of some sort, were the graves, all in a row, of seven or eight of the men killed in that fight, with the headboards giving the name and regiment of each. Nearby was the little shelter tent still standing in which it was said young Fish of Colonel Wood's regiment had died.[7] From this point on, clear to the river on whose banks we pitched our tents that night, were the unmistakable signs of war and the presence of an army. On every slight elevation in the general waste of cactus and rank vegetation could be seen the abandoned shelter of some body of soldiers—the forked sticks covered with brush, or a poncho or a blanket; or a small clearing cut out of the jungle; the remains of the little fires at which they had boiled their coffee, and the beds of brush and leaves on which they had slept. On both sides of the road the ground was thickly strewn with the debris so familiar to those who have followed in the wake of an army on the march. There were broken-down wagons, dumped into the ditch or the bed of a creek and abandoned. Once in a while there was a dead mule, faithful, patient, tireless, calumniated, kicking friend of the hungry soldier, unburied, unmarked, unsung, and unattended save by the score or two of fat repulsive vultures, scavengers of Cuba, that perched on his skeleton. There were blankets, ponchos, hats, coats, belts, canteens, haversacks, cooking utensils, buckles, straps, empty tin cans, now and then the remains of a box of hardtack tramped into the mud, and the little mounds just outside of the trail with the ominous headboard made of a crackerbox cover, with the name and company and regiment of some poor boy who had been killed or died of disease—all the flotsam and jetsam of war.

We met many wounded men going back to Siboney, some in the great lumbering army wagons, looking as if they were suffering the torments of the damned, from the awful jolting, some on horseback, and some dragging themselves along on foot, but all cheerful and uncomplaining and telling us to hurry up and get there in time to help finish up the Dons.

When about a mile out of Siboney, General Henry halted until the head of the column overtook him. He there informed the regimental commander that he would ride ahead to corps headquarters and report, and receive General Shafter's further orders as to our disposition; and that, having done this, he would meet us on the road and give us our instructions. He, then, with his staff, forged ahead, and we saw no more of him until we reached the spot where we encamped.

Between five and six o'clock, when within half a mile of the Aguadores River, we met Major Mills, assistant adjutant general on General Henry's staff, who delivered to the commanding officer an order from General Henry to put his regiment into camp at a designated spot a short distance ahead. Major Mills stated that he had been sent back to deliver the order and to conduct the regiment to the ground selected. In the conversation that ensued, while marching along, Major Mills informed the commanding officer that General Henry and his staff had ridden up to Shafter's headquarters, some two or three miles in advance, where he had reported, and announced that the Eighth Ohio was approaching, and had received an order from General Shafter to put us into camp for the night on the east bank of the Aguadores River.

When we had marched over the intervening distance General Henry met us in the road, pointed out the ground, and reiterated the order to the commanding officer to encamp the regiment there. The general had already pitched his tents. Together the general and the regimental commander inspected the grounds, and he made some suggestions about guards, water, etc., and as the different battalions came in they were directed where to go and in what manner to pitch their tents. That camp was very appropriately named the next morning by the boys, Camp Mud.

That night it rained. To the peaceful citizen of northern Ohio that does not seem a very significant statement. It frequently rains there and the world seems to be the better for it. But in a tropical climate where the rainfall is anywhere from eight to twenty-five feet per annum, and when a fellow has to go to bed with his umbrella raised and his galoshes on, and it rained all the time, to refer to any particular date and say that on that day it rained signifies something out of the ordinary. The climate of Cuba calls to mind the incident of the gentleman of color, who, being brought before a magistrate, was asked if he was addicted to the use of intoxicating liquors, and replied, "Well, sah! I'se not in de habit o' drinking whiskey o'ny on two 'casions. One is when I'se washin' sheep, and de oder is when I isn't washin' sheep!" The year in Cuba is divided into two seasons, the "rainy season" and the "dry season." The only distinction is that in the dry season it rains all the time, and in the rainy season it rains a good deal more.

Very soon after dark the rain came down in its most approved tropical style. Officers and men plunged into their little shelter tents like a village full of prairie dogs popping into their holes at an alarm. The storm increased in intensity very rapidly, and was accompanied by the most brilliant electrical display and the most terrific thunder any of us had ever seen or heard. The flashes of lightning would start in away off in the east and rush along the mountain tops like a train of fire, and disappear in the west. Then would follow the awful explosions and the deep roar of thunder that fairly made the earth shake under us. These were so continuous that men could hardly carry on conversation while the electrical disturbance lasted. At first it seemed as if that lightning would certainly tear everything to pieces in Santiago, and everybody hugged the ground to avoid exposure. At length, however, it became an old story and many stood outside their shelters to witness the scene. And the rain! There was no wind, and all the water had to do was to come right straight down and find a place to fall on. In Ohio when we have that kind of a rain lasting ten or fifteen minutes, we call it a cloudburst. That rain of July 11 was a cloudburst lasting six or eight hours and tapering off into a respectable shower toward morning. It was phenomenal even for that aqueous latitude. Everybody and everything was in water, or under water, or surrounded by water.

The situation, however, was not altogether destitute of humor. Most of the officers, before leaving the States, had been beguiled by the soft blandishments of a young gentleman from Michigan into supplying themselves with an ingenious device for a sleeping place when they reached the hot and humid isle. It was entitled a "hammock." It was a hammock made of canvas, with guys and stays and uprights and pegs. It was an easy proposition. You just put this upright here, and this one at the other end; then you drove you this peg in the ground—so; tie this rope to the peg, then tie this rope to a peg at the other end—so; and there you have it. Then you get right into it, this way; lie down, pull the mosquito netting over your face, close your eyes, and you are as cool and comfortable and restful as Cleopatra was with half a dozen naked Nubian gentlemen standing around and fanning her with peacock feathers while she sipped her mandragora.

That hammock would hold all you could put into it. We knew it would, because the smooth-faced young villain from Kalamazoo said it would; besides he demonstrated the fact clearly at Camp Alger. He got Captain Critchfield and Surgeon Smith, the featherweights of the regiment—total weight, 560 pounds—into the seductive stretcher, and the thing stood as solid as the everlasting hills.

It received its initiation that night. When the rains began to descend the young gentlemen who had hammocks climbed into them, rolled themselves in their blankets, stretched their ponchos over them, embraced themselves for having displayed such foresight, and commiserated the rest of us because we were forced to sleep on the ground. Along about ten or eleven o'clock the soil had become thoroughly saturated, the wet ropes began to tighten up, the pegs slipped out of the mushy ground, and the hammocks began to tumble. From that on at short intervals could be heard the swish of the guys as they pulled the pegs out of the ground, and splash and the scream as some fellow went down into the water, and then the great shout of laughter all over the camp, and the cries of "How's your hammock?"

The tents, also, went down rapidly, and more than half the regiment stood around in the mud and water, or, if they were fortunate, sat on boulders or tomato cans, soaked to the skin, waiting for morning. That night is known in the history of the campaign in Santiago as "The night it rained."

When morning came the streams were swift-flowing torrents and the roads were under water and almost bottomless. An orderly from General Shafter came over early in the forenoon with instructions for the Eighth Regiment to remain in the camp then occupied until further orders. By the time the roads became passable negotiations were in progress for the surrender of the Spanish, a truce was declared, and of course no movements of troops could be made.

There were no organized bodies of troops between us and Siboney, only stragglers and detachments going after or returning with supplies, and we did not know what was in front of us or in the hills on either flank. After consultation with General Henry, therefore, a strong picket guard was thrown out in every direction, Captain E. L. Gyger of Company K acting as officer of the day, and the officers and men were instructed where and how to form in case of an alarm. Early in the evening one of the picket posts fired on what they supposed was a squad of men, who fled at once. Aside from this there was no disturbance except that caused by the elements, but everybody who went up or down the country was halted and made to show his character or be brought into camp. Among those halted was Mr. Honoré F. Lainé, a correspondent of a New York daily, who was on his way to Siboney with dispatches for his paper when he was held up by our pickets. In relating the circumstance afterward and commenting on the general looseness he remarked that before the surrender he had been able to go inside the Spanish lines and anywhere inside of our lines without being called on to show his credentials, until he struck the Eighth Ohio.

On the evening of the twelfth General Henry advised the regimental commander that he had been ordered by General Shafter to proceed to Siboney early the next morning and with the Sixth Illinois, Sixth Massachusetts, and some other regiment then on transports off Siboney, and a battery of artillery, to sail down below the entrance to Santiago Bay, land on the west side of the bay, and drive back the Spanish force encamped there, the purpose being to create a diversion and demonstrate to the Dons the advisability of surrendering before their city was bombarded. When it was suggested that he take the Eighth with him on the expedition he replied that he had made the same suggestion to General Shafter, but the general said that the vessel owners or captains would not allow any troops to be taken on board from the island, because they were infected with yellow fever. Even General Henry with his staff had considerable difficulty in boarding one of the steamers, and was compelled to use strategy and "bluff" before he succeeded. He left us about half past five o'clock in the morning of the thirteenth.

That same day a little episode occurred that was not calculated to cause the memory of the commanding general to be enshrined in the hearts of the Eighth. The day before, when it became apparent that we would be held somewhere in that immediate vicinity for some days, two parties were sent out to explore for a better location for a camp than Camp Mud. Captain Critchfield and Surgeon Wuchter went in one direction, and Captain Charlton and Lieutenant Bradford in another. The camp we then occupied was sure to breed disease. It had been occupied only a few days before by cavalry or artillery or both, and was filthy when we filed into it. A rain of ten or twelve hours, and the tread of 1,300 men confined in such a narrow space, had transformed it into a quagmire. It was a low-level, mucky cactus field; and when the sun came out and beat down on that muck the stench from the decaying vegetation stirred up by the ceaseless tramp of the men was sickening. Nothing but the interposition of Divine Providence could prevent an outbreak of sickness.

The little performance grew partly out of the desire to move the camp, and as some versions of it have been given that were not accurate it will not be inappropriate to make a correct statement of the occurrence a part of this "Story of the Eighth." It took place in an interview between General Shafter and the commanding officer of the Eighth, and for that reason the use of the personal pronoun in relating the circumstance will not be deemed a display of egotism.

At about ten minutes before six o'clock, on the morning of the thirteenth, an orderly rode up to the headquarters of the regiment and handed me an order of which the following is a copy.

Headquarters, V Army Corps
July 13, 1898

To the Commanding Officer
Eighth Ohio Volunteer Infantry

The commanding general directs you send forward one battalion of your regiment at once to encamp at these headquarters. This battalion will be retained here until further orders.

Very respectfully,
E. J. McClernand
Assistant adjutant general

The hour fixed for Reveille was six o'clock but regimental bugler Fulton was at once routed out and directed to sound the call. At the same time an orderly was sent to Major Weybrecht with instructions for him to report at headquarters immediately, which he did within two or three minutes, completing his toilet as he came. The order was shown to him and he was directed to have his men cook their coffee at once, roll their shelter tents and blankets, form as rapidly as possible and march over to corps headquarters.

At the same time the orderly delivered the above order he handed me a note from General Shafter directing me to report to him at his quarters in person. After a hasty breakfast of hardtack and coffee, and some further instructions to Major Weybrecht about hurrying up his men, I started on foot for General Shafter's camp, some two miles distant. As I passed behind the trees at the river a glance back at the camp showed the companies of the battalion forming and the first one marching out into the road. The major and his men were pleased with the order to move and were going at it with ardor. This was about half past six o'clock. I reached General Shafter's camp about twenty minutes after seven. After some delay I found the general's tent, designated by a headquarters flag, and saw an officer seated in front of it whom I at once recognized as General Shafter from the pictures I had seen of him. He was seated in a large camp chair with a high canvas back. He was without a coat; his shirt, a sort of "hickory" affair, was worn décolleté in a degree that would have displayed the most ravishing charms of the ballet dancer, if he had possessed them, and the sleeves were turned up. His head was without a cover, and the condition of his hair created a suspicion that his "valley" had not yet appeared upon the scene of action. His left foot and leg, heavily bandaged, rested upon a cracker box. On the other foot he wore a Brussels carpet slipper with a cheap, slouchy, coarse-looking sock hanging down over it. In his hand he held a fan of the palm-leaf variety with which he was vigorously trying to create an artificial zephyr. All this was perhaps admissible, as the environment was not favorable to the observance of the customs of polite society in the matter of dress. But he was not pretty. His most ardent admirers have never likened him to Adonis or Hyperion.

I approached within respectful distance, saluted, and said, "This is General Shafter, I believe?"

He replied, "Yes, sir!"

"I am Colonel Hard of the Eighth Ohio, and I report in obedience to your orders."

"All right, colonel. Take a seat!"

I removed my hat and sat down on an empty cracker box to which he pointed. Then turning to me without further preliminaries he blurted out,

"Where in hell is that battalion I ordered you to send over here?" This nearly knocked the wind out of me, but I recovered myself and replied:

"It's on the way, sir!"

"Well, how long does it take one of your G—d d——d militia battalions to march two miles?"

"Ordinarily, sir, they could march it in about thirty minutes, but the river is high, the roads are bad, and they are obliged to break into column of twos or even single file part of the way, so that it may take them somewhat longer."

"Well we marched over that trail, and I don't see why in hell you can't do it."

"No, sir! There is no reason why they can't march it. I think they will be here in a few minutes, as they were starting when I left camp."

Then he returned to the assault along a new line.

"I don't know what in hell you're here for anyway! I don't want any of your G—d d——d militia around me!"

"Well I don't know, sir! Only that when you called for reinforcements the other day, the War Department ordered us here, and we obeyed orders."

"How many men have you?"

"Thirteen hundred."

"How are you armed?"

"Springfield rifles."

"How much ammunition?"

"Two hundred rounds."

"Well, I'll give you something to do. If the Spaniards don't surrender tomorrow I'll give you some marching and shooting to do."

"All right, sir! We will go wherever you order us. We were disappointed to be halted the other night before getting up to the trenches."

After a little further conversation that branch of the subject seemed to be disposed of, and the general referred to my request of the day before for permission to move our camp.

"Yes," I said, "if it will not interfere with the duty you want us to perform I would like to change our camp."

"What do you want to move your camp for?"

I explained the situation and conditions of the camp and expressed fear that they would very soon cause a great deal of sickness.

"Where do you want to move to?"

I described two locations that our officers had visited, only a few hundred yards from Camp Mud, and no farther from corps headquarters, either of which was higher ground and in many respects much more desirable. One of these was Sevilla Hill.

"Well I don't want you there."

Then calling an officer of his staff he inquired,

"Captain, do you know where the Eighth Ohio is encamped?"

"Yes, sir. It's on the ground where the ——th regiment was encamped."

"Isn't that a good camping ground?"

"Why, it was all right when they were there."

Then turning to me the general said, "If they could put up with that I guess you can. Your men are not a d——d bit better than ours. You need not move your camp."

"All right, sir!"

After a moment, however, he again addressed his staff officer, who was a captain of engineers—and a gentleman, by the way—and inquired if a good spot for a camp could not be found at a certain point which he designated, and after discussing the matter with him for a few moments directed him to accompany me and point out the position, and authorized me, if it was found desirable, to move to that place.

Just at this point a staff officer approached, saluted, and reported that "That battalion you ordered over from the Eighth Ohio is here. What shall I do with it?"

"You may hold it there for the present. I'll let you know a little later."

And that battalion stood there in the hot sun until ten o'clock waiting for orders. That was all right. Nobody objected, and they would have stood there all day, cheerfully, without a word of complaint, if it had been necessary. But the fact indicated that there was no emergency that justified the commanding general in employing the abuse and brutality he did, because Major Weybrecht had not hurried his men over there at double-time without breakfast.

Then I ventured to inquire if he could give me a couple of wagons to move the 3rd Battalion's luggage over with. "What in h——l do you want wagons for?"

I explained what they had to move, which I assumed they ought to bring with them as they were ordered to encamp there "until further orders." This was principally the cooking outfit which had been brought up the night before, some sick men's luggage, and a few who were already too ill to walk.

"They've no business to have anything they can't carry on their shoulders. Let them carry it on their backs. We carried all our stuff on our backs, and your men can do the same!"

"All right, sir!"

As there seemed to be no further business before the lodge I arose and asked, "Is that all, sir?," and receiving an affirmative answer I thanked the general for his courtesy and withdrew. As I was moving off he called and asked me how many wagons I wanted.

"I don't want any, sir!"

Then addressing another officer he said, "Can you give the colonel a couple of wagons?"

I interposed and said, "Now, general, I don't want to put you to any inconvenience, and if you have no transportation to spare, we will get along without it."

The officer replied, "Oh, we can give you all the wagons you want, just as well as not."

"You may send two wagons over to report to Colonel Hard of the Eighth Ohio," said General Shafter.

I saluted and walked away with the staff officer.[8]

After leaving corps headquarters we crawled through the jungle and underbrush, so dense that we had to bend nearly double and part it with our hands, crossed the river a couple of times, and at length came to the spot suggested for a new camp. It was no better than the old one, in fact it was worse in many respects, and it was within a few rods of the hospital camp which had at the entrance on the opposite side a warning sign, "Yellow fever hospital, keep out."

I determined not to move to that place, and the staff officer agreed with me that it would not be a wise selection.

We remained in Camp Mud. I returned to camp carrying a considerable weight of indignation concealed beneath my blouse, and wondering if the coarse, profane, and brutal assault from which I had just escaped was characteristic of "a soldier and a gentleman." As I walked along reflecting on the interview the one thing that floated constantly before my mental vision and would not down was the form of that matchless warrior Sir John Falstaff, with the pregnant description of character supplied by his biographer—"Gross, open, palpable."

In striking contrast with the bullying of Shafter was the bearing of General Miles. The next day after the occurrence related above—July 14—the general passed through our camp, with an escort of cavalry, on his way over to General Shafter's headquarters. He halted and spent a few minutes at regimental headquarters in conversation, inquiring about the health of officers and men.[9]

Again on the fifteenth, after the surrender, on his way to Siboney, accompanied by Richard Harding Davis, and his staff of course, he rode through our camp.[10] He stopped at headquarters, where he told us of the surrender concluded only a little time before, and related in some detail the terms of the capitulation, the number of men and the territory included in the arrangement, the arms, etc. He stated that he was going to Siboney, whence he would sail with his expedition to Puerto Rico in a few days. In response to a suggestion he agreed to take the Eighth to rejoin our brigade and accompany the expedition to Puerto Rico if he could possibly get us onto a transport.[11]

Akron depot, embarkation point for the Eighth Ohio. (*Art Work of Akron,* 1898.)

A few of the boys. (U.S. Army Military History Institute.)

The Eighth at the ready, Camp Alger. (Library of Congress stereograph collection.)

Charles W. F. Dick, lieutenant colonel of the regiment.

Tentmates show off their new home.

Camp Alger's guard quarters.

Guard mount at Camp Alger.

"The best beloved character in the regiment," Chaplain I. N. Kieffer.

Regimental hospital for the Eighth Ohio. (The Western Reserve Historical Society.)

Setting off from Camp Alger to enlist recruits. (The Western Reserve Historical Society.)

Inspection, Camp Alger. (The Western Reserve Historical Society.)

Rookies who joined the Eighth Ohio. (The Western Reserve Historical Society.)

Messmates at Camp Alger.

Company B's cook house.

Men of the Eighth out for a swim. (The Western Reserve Historical Society.)

Horse tent of the Eighth Ohio, Camp Alger.

A teamster with his wagon and army mules.

Breaking camp for assignment to Cuba. (Library of Congress stereograph collection.)

The Eighth Ohio ready to leave for Cuba. (Library of Congress stereograph collection.)

Loading wagons for the move. (National Archives.)

He again also inquired about the health of the regiment, and taking advantage of the opportunity I asked permission to move the regiment out of the miserable camp it then occupied. He inquired if there were any better locations near, and I pointed to the hill on our south, saying that an examination had demonstrated that it was an excellent spot for an encampment though a little difficult of access. He at once gave me permission to move up onto Sevilla Hill, and made some commendatory allusion to the anxiety evinced in caring for the physical condition of the regiment. Before the sun went down a part of one battalion was on top of that hill, and the balance of the regiment followed the next morning.

There is not the slightest doubt that the seeds of disease were sown in that camp on the banks of the river, which afterward developed into the epidemic that took hold of us on the hill. Much of it might have been avoided if we had been allowed to move when we first requested permission. Without good reason General Shafter refused the permission. Possibly his conscience has since pricked him sometimes—I hope his heart has never ached as mine did when my boys were dying, one, two and sometimes four a day.

VI

Fever

On the eleventh of July, as we marched out of Siboney, the commanding officer was quietly informed that among the sick in the hospitals at that point there were some thirty cases which the surgeons pronounced yellow fever. To avoid creating alarm among the men, Surgeon Major Farquhar who had learned the fact from the hospital surgeons was directed to say nothing about it. The next report we had, on the thirteenth, was that there were more than a hundred cases of yellow fever and that General Miles had ordered the town to be burned. On the fourteenth the number had grown to three hundred, and on the nineteenth the reports showed over nine hundred cases at that place. The physical condition of the army had become alarming. Twenty-five percent of the men were in the extemporized hospitals and fifty percent of the whole army was unfit for duty. The wagons going down to Siboney were filled with gaunt, hollow-eyed yellow boys, shaking their teeth out with chills or burning with fever, too weak to help themselves, jolted and jerked from one side to the other, but always hanging to their rifles and always brave. There was a constant procession, too, of sick men on foot, each aided by a comrade or two, who would walk a few rods and then lie down to rest and gather strength for another rush. The nerve of these sick boys was simply magnificent. There was no whining or complaining. As one young soldier of the Sixth Infantry said, "Oh, of course I'm feeling pretty tough just now, but I'll be all right in a day or two." One man driving a four-mule team fell off his mule, just as he was going through our camp. Some of our boys picked him up, carried him into camp, and fixed a bed for him under a tree where he remained for two or three hours a very sick man. When he was able to sit up he was determined to take his team and drive on, and nothing would dissuade him. "Why I've *got* to go," he said. "I'm ordered to get this team in by six o'clock." He started but after going a few rods he went down again.

He was again made comfortable, a detail sent in with his team, to relieve his mind, and an ambulance sent for to carry him to the hospital.[1]

On the nineteenth of July an order came to the commanding officer of the Eighth directing him to place the regiment in isolation for a period of ten days at the end of which time, if our physical condition was satisfactory, we were to be sent to join our brigade then about sailing for Puerto Rico. The order directed that a sufficient guard should be placed about the camp to enforce the observance of the quarantine; that neither officers nor men should be allowed to visit Siboney or Santiago except in case of urgent necessity; and that they should avoid contact with the frequent parties of natives going up and down the trails. The medical board also added some requirements regarding sanitation, boiling the drinking water, abstention from eating native fruits, etc.

These restrictions were all imposed by General Shafter's order for the good of the men of the regiment—not to gratify any desire of his to be tyrannical, as some sensational correspondents would have made it appear. In the first place it was hoped that by this course we would escape the yellow fever with which at that time we were apparently not infected. Then if we avoided the infection it would enable us to go to Puerto Rico, which it was generally conceded is a much more healthful climate. Moreover if we could succeed in getting to Puerto Rico we could enjoy the rare distinction of being the only organization in the army to participate in the subjugation of both islands. The order was promulgated and explained to the men. The officers, certainly, and probably most of the men, were anxious to win the advantages that were likely to follow a strict observance of the order. It is fair to say that had it been possible to strictly enforce the quarantine we would in all probability have gone to Puerto Rico. But there were a few men in the regiment who evaded or disobeyed the orders, which they seemed to consider an abridgement of their personal liberty. There were frequent—almost daily—communications from General Shafter calling attention to the presence of Eighth Ohio men in the city without permission, and in violation of the orders, and admonishing the commanding officer that these orders must be more rigidly enforced. As a result at the expiration of the period of isolation the condition of the regiment was such and the commanding general's recollection of the violations of the quarantine so fresh that the prejudice was against us rather than in our favor. And yet, on the return of the regiment to the States, some of the yellow journals took up this matter and made the effort to enforce these orders the basis of charges of cruelty and tyranny against the commanding officer.

On the seventeenth of July, Captain Wuchter, assistant surgeon, and then with the 3rd Battalion, was ordered by the commanding general to report for duty to the commanding officer of the 33rd Michigan. One of the medical officers of that regiment was sick or dead, and the others it was reported had suffered an attack of "buck fever" and gone home. Surgeon Wuchter was given charge of the entire regiment, and when he was relieved August 9 to return to his regiment he brought with him a very highly commendatory letter from the colonel of the 33rd.

Captain Wuchter's detachment left the 3rd Battalion of our regiment without a medical officer. One of the remaining surgeons and a hospital steward visited the battalion almost daily, but the service was not sufficient, and moreover it was more than they could bear up under. A request was therefore made to the corps surgeon for a detail of a contract physician, which was promised us. It was not, however, until the third of August that Dr. John Carling was sent to report to Major Weybrecht. Dr. Carling was a surgeon at the Riverside Hospital, New York City. He volunteered his services in June and was sent to Santiago in the latter part of July, on the *Olivette,* the same transport that brought Chaplain Campbell. He was faithful, energetic and efficient, and endeared himself to the men of the 3rd Battalion and to the officers of the entire regiment.

The period of isolation prescribed terminated on the thirtieth of July. We had a great many sick in the regiment but up to that time we had buried but one man—Corporal William R. Knowles of Company K, who died on the evening of the twenty-eighth. The death and burial of Knowles left an indelible impression on the regiment. It was deemed best to bury the body at once. An orderly was sent to Major Weybrecht, to whose battalion he belonged, notifying him that the interment would take place as soon as the preparations could be made. A detail of men was put to work with the boards from an accumulation of hardtack boxes, and the rude implements at hand, to construct a coffin, while another squad dug the grave under a little clump of trees a few rods east of the camp. The ominous clank of the hammers in the hands of the carpenters, and the thud of the picks in the hard, stony ground, in the stillness of the night, went resounding through the camp with provoking distinctness. Company K with its officers and the battalion officers came over from the 3rd Battalion camp an hour before the preparations were complete, splashing through the mud and water, and swishing through the tall grass, and there was all the hurrying and suppressed conversation that prevails in the presence of death. Just at midnight the little procession, limited to his own company for various good reasons, picked up the rude coffin and moved out to the place of sepulture. We had no chaplain, and the commanding officer read the brief and impressive service from the Protestant Episcopal prayer book, by the flickering light of a candle sputtering in the wind; the significant words, "Earth to earth, dust to dust," were pronounced; the shallow grave was filled, and the little column retraced its steps. There was no volley over the grave, no bugle sounded the customary Taps. It was a weird scene, recalling vividly to many minds the familiar couplet of our schoolboy days:

Not a drum was heard, not a funeral note
As his corpse to the rampart we hurried:
Not a soldier discharged his farewell shot
O'er the grave where our hero we buried.

We buried him darkly at dead of night;
The sods with our bayonets turning;
By the struggling moonbeam's misty light,
And the lantern dimly burning.

Between this date, July 28, and the day on which our newly appointed chaplain, Reverend J. O. Campbell, arrived, August 3, seven more of our men died and were buried on Sevilla Hill. Private Harry Hague of Company H died July 31, and Leonard L. Weiker of the same company died August 1. Both of these young men were bright, intelligent, well-educated, and of excellent character with fine prospects in life, and both of them were sons of personal friends of the commanding officer of the regiment and the officers of their company. Three others died on the first of August, Privates Amos G. Simpson of Company M, Mansfield; Edward S. Wingerter of Company I, Canton; and Arthur Nelson of Company B, Akron; making four on that day. On the second there were two deaths, Privates Charles C. Kiplinger of Company A, Bucyrus, and Charles F. Miller of Company C of Ashland. These were all buried in the regimental cemetery on the hill, with the same simple services, sometimes conducted by the commanding officer, sometimes by Major Vollrath, and sometimes by Major Bryan. In each grave was placed a tightly sealed bottle containing a slip of paper on which was recorded the name, company, age, and date of death of the dead soldier, and at the head of each grave a rudely carved headboard, made from a cracker box, containing the same data. The graves of all the dead who were buried by our own boys were similarly marked for identification. While the material lasted the comrades of the dead always placed them in one of the rude coffins; when it was exhausted they constructed a bed of boughs and leaves, and a cover of branches and twigs, and the body, wrapped in his blanket, and clothed in the soldier's garb he had worn in life, was tenderly lowered into his shallow grave.[2]

During that period of sickness and death and burials the good qualities of the men who had hearts under their blouses came out strong. Great big, husky, bearded, rough-looking men ministered to their sick comrades as tenderly and devotedly as a mother with her helpless child, and without tears, but with as much gentleness, stood by or aided in the burial. A thousand times daily as this devotion was displayed came up the thought, "Greater love than this hath no man."

Chaplain Campbell arrived in camp on the morning of August 3 and thereafter took charge, of course, of all matters of this kind. Although personally known to only a few of the officers and men he received a hearty greeting. After a hurried introduction and a brief explanation of the situation, he pulled on his rubber boots and rubber coat and started out in the rain and mud to cheer the sick and get acquainted with the well. Inside of two or three hours he had said something to every man, and from that time until the end of his service he was busy caring for the sick, comforting the dying, and burying the dead.[3]

Before we left the island to return to the States fourteen more deaths occurred in the Eighth, eight of them at Sevilla Hill and six at Siboney. Privates William K. Adams and Moses McDowell of Company H died at Sevilla Hill August 3 and Sergeant Charles Thoman of Company A, Bucyrus, at the same place August 4. On the fifth Private George Coleman, of Company M, died at Sevilla, and Private Frank Gibler of Company I died and was buried at Siboney. There were three deaths again on the seventh of August, all of them at Siboney: Privates George L. Happer, of Millersburg, of Company H, Ora N. Royer of Company K, Alliance, and Corporal Dudley Wilson of Company G, Wadsworth. Captain John A. Leininger of Company F had been unfit for duty much of the time after landing but never went to the hospital. At length on the seventh of August it was thought best to send him into Santiago to the officers' hospital where it was thought he could have better care. We were shocked on the evening of the eighth when his colored servant came into camp with the news that his captain was dead. The officers of his company, with a detail of men, at once went into the city and carefully interred the remains in the Santiago cemetery.

Private Ebbie Bland of Company A died on the eleventh of August at Siboney. Private Irwin Lautzenheiser of Company D, Wooster, died at Sevilla Hill August 13. His brother, also a member of Company D, was with him during his sickness and at his death, which occurred only a few days before our departure for the north. Corporal John S. Lee of Company G, a cousin of Captain Lee, died August 15 at Siboney, and on the sixteenth Corporal Charles E. Tarner of Company L died in the camp on San Juan Hill, only a few hours before the orders for our embarkation were delivered. He was buried in the trenches—one of the last things the men of his company did before starting into the city. The next day before we went on board the *Mohawk* we learned that Ward A. Wilford of Akron, a member of Company B, had died on the sixteenth at Siboney. This made a total of twenty-two men whose bodies we left on the island of Cuba as we sailed away, the Eighth Ohio's contribution to its freedom from Spanish domination.

The death rate was not alarming. But the sickness was appalling. The percentage of sick reported each day by the regiments varied all the way from twenty to forty. Of those not reported sick a very large proportion were weak, emaciated, and unfit for duty. It is safe to say that if the emergency had arisen not five thousand men in that whole army could have marched five miles and carried their accouterments and a single day's rations. Just what ailed us it is difficult for us laymen to determine when the doctors disagreed so widely. Our surgeons did not believe it was yellow fever, and in this opinion they were supported by many, perhaps a majority of the surgeons on the island. But by whatever name it may be designated it was an exceedingly debilitating and depressing ailment. Its victims lost appetite, ambition, and sometimes nerve. Many were afflicted with dementia of various degrees, and there were not a few sad cases of extreme insanity. And then there was before us continually the fear that after the whole army had become exhausted and enervated by this fever, whatever it was, when September came the genuine, unadulterated, sure-enough yellow fever would assail us, and then no man would have the physical strength to withstand the siege.

As early as the twenty-fifth of July the problem of what to do with that army at Santiago was agitating the authorities at Washington. At one time it was proposed to move it to North Carolina, but the newspapers announced that the patriotic governor of that state would call out his militia and prevent the landing. Then the coast of Maine was suggested, and at length the eastern end of Long Island. It was designed to transport the army to some healthful spot where it might recuperate and be ready for the movement against Havana when cool and dry weather arrived. General Shafter and his medical adviser represented to the government the gravity of the situation. This was about the condition of affairs when the term of the Eighth's isolation expired.[4]

On the evening of the first day of August the following cablegram was received by the commanding officer of the regiment:

Washington, August 1, 1898

Colonel Hard
Eighth Ohio Volunteers
Santiago

Confer with General Shafter, and if it is certain that your regiment is entirely free from fever it is possible we will be able to get you to Puerto Rico but you would not have us take any chances of inoculating the army there with fever.

H. C. Corbin
Adjutant General

It was too late to see General Shafter that evening. On the morning of the second of August, armed with the medical reports of the regiment of the day before, I went in to the city and reported to the commanding general. After a conference of an hour with him in which he discussed the conditions fully and secured all the information obtainable he suggested that he would look further into the matter and reach a conclusion after luncheon. At the second interview at which the corps surgeon, Major Harvard, was present, and submitted his reports regarding our physical condition, General Shafter said that we were unfit to go to Puerto Rico, that in fact there was not a regiment on the island that was fit for duty; that it would be worse than folly to send us there; that the proper thing to do with us was to send us north where we could recuperate; that he had advised the War Department that it ought to take the whole army out of Cuba at once, and that if it was not done one half the army would never leave the island alive. He then called a stenographer and dictated a cablegram to the adjutant general in substance as follows:

> Have conferred with Colonel Hard as directed. His regiment wholly unfit to go to Puerto Rico. More than three hundred sick. Will take half men of regiment to take care of other half. I suggest the regiment ought to be sent north at once to recuperate.

The commanding officer of the Eighth reported to Adjutant General Corbin the result of the conference, as follows:

> Have conferred with General Shafter as directed. He pronounces regiment unfit to go to Puerto Rico, and advises that it be sent north. If this is done it should be at once.

The general opinion among the officers about Santiago then was that the troops would all be sent to Florida or Carolina when withdrawn from Cuba. The prospect seemed favorable for getting out of the fever climate.

On returning to camp in the evening it transpired that during the day the medical commission had visited our regiment and made a thorough examination. Before leaving they announced to Lieutenant Colonel Dick the result, which was that they had found nine clearly defined cases of yellow fever, and they stated that they would so report to headquarters. This was something of a blow, as it meant that like the rest of the army we had the dreaded fever, and that we certainly could not go to Puerto Rico, and probably not to the States. After a conference with the field officers it was concluded that our only hope of getting out of Cuba soon lay in prevailing on Major Kennedy, the surgeon who made the examination, to modify his report so far as it related to the yellow fever. Lieutenant Colonel Dick, Surgeon Major Farquhar, and Major Weybrecht were directed to go over to Major Kennedy's quarters some four miles distant, immediately after mess the next morning, for the purpose of securing from him such a modification of his report. Our surgeons still protested that we had no yellow fever.

On the morning of August 3 these officers rode over to Major Kennedy's quarters and urged him to comply with our wishes in the matter, laying stress upon the fact that there was considerable doubt and diversity of opinion as to the real character of the disease. When they returned toward evening they reported that their mission had failed.

On the morning of that same day, August 3, while these officers were trying to secure a withdrawal of the report that we had yellow fever, matters suddenly and somewhat unexpectedly reached a climax. An order by cable reached General Shafter from the Secretary of War, on the recommendation of Surgeon General Sternberg, directing him to move the entire army into the interior where the land was higher and it was thought the conditions were more favorable for its health. This soon became known everywhere in the camps, and produced a terrible feeling of despondency throughout the army. There was a general sentiment that we were to be left there to our fate and that V Corps would lose half its men before it ever set foot again on the soil of the United States. This feeling was not confined to any class or rank. Generals and privates, soldiers and civilian employees, regulars and volunteers—everybody was astounded at what seemed to be before them.

The medical officers protested that the movement would be disastrous, as the conditions in the interior, instead of being better, were far worse than on the coast. A meeting of all general officers—all officers commanding brigades and divisions—was at once called, and the famous "round robin" was formulated. It was addressed to General Shafter, and signed by all these officers, the signatures, it was said, being affixed in the form of a circle so that no one should appear to have signed it first. At all events it was signed and presented. This was immediately cabled to the Secretary of War. It created consternation in government circles and throughout the country. It was an act that crowded closely upon insubordination. If it had been instigated and signed by a lot of volunteer officers it would have been held up by some of the "regulars" as another evidence of the utter incompetency and lack of discipline of "them volunteers." But it produced results. The order to get the army out of Cuba came just as fast as the cable could bring it. In his official report of the campaign in Santiago, General Shafter says, "On August 4th I received orders to begin the embarkation of my command and ship them to Montauk Point, Long Island, New York."[5]

From that moment all efforts were turned toward getting the men into condition so that we would leave a minimum number of sick behind. It was quietly determined to take every man along on board as "well" who could stand upright long enough to walk across the gangplank. Soon after the order to move the army north was issued, General Shafter granted permission to move our camp up into the outskirts of the city, giving us carte blanche to select our own ground. A suitable location was found just inside the original line of entrenchments on San Juan Hill, on the south side of the Siboney road. We had several streams to ford, some of them difficult, before reaching the city. Lieutenants Yost and Brosius were detailed with a corps of engineers, consisting of forty men, to build bridges across the most difficult. On the morning of the tenth, the day on which we moved in, this detail left camp about three o'clock, and by the time the troops began to march, about seven o'clock, they had bridged every stream. A rear guard of thirty men under command of Lieutenant Hard followed the column, to pick up stragglers, look after any who might be taken sick, gather up abandoned luggage, etc. Before they reached the city the few wagons and horses at command were loaded down with rolls and men who had succumbed to the heat and the march.

When we left Sevilla Hill, Surgeon Major Farquhar remained at that place with a sufficient detail to care for the sick who were unable to march or could not be moved. Major Weybrecht's battalion moved up from its camp near Shafter's headquarters, a little later in the day, going into camp near the other two battalions. The regiment was once more encamped in a body. Dr. Carling was left behind with a detail in charge of the sick of the 3rd Battalion in their old camp. An effort was made to move these sick either to the corps hospitals or to join their command, and the corps surgeon was appealed to for ambulances or even wagons but with indifferent success. One of the surgeons begged for two ambulances but the best he could get was a vague promise of one ambulance as soon as it could be spared—probably in a day or two. Then he pleaded for an army wagon. But an order had been issued against allowing sick men to ride in the wagons, for fear they would infect the subsistence which was carried in them. Then the commanding officer tried his hand, and was in a fair way to receive the same "cold turndown," when a suggestion that if satisfaction could not be obtained there it would be necessary to go farther up toward the head of the procession brought the answer and two ambulances. One of these was "seized" by somebody before we had made the second trip with it. Gradually, however, the sick in these two camps were disposed of, and at the time of the order to sail nearly all of them had been removed.

Some of the severest experiences of the brief campaign were those of the sick men being brought up to the city from these camps. Two members of Company B—Privates Wilford and Cline—gave out in the march and had gone only to the San Juan River when night overtook them and [they] were compelled to encamp there for the night in the rain and mud. When morning came they climbed into a wagon going toward the city, but the wagon upset in midstream and they narrowly escaped drowning. The exposure of that night in the rain and cold, and the ducking in the stream, aggravated their illness, and Wilford died a few days afterward.

Four or five times in that two weeks orders came to the commanding officer to hold his regiment in readiness to embark the next day or in two days, but the order to march did not materialize.

Shortly after the removal of the quarantine restrictions the Eighth was attached to a brigade composed of the First Illinois, First District of Columbia, and the Eighth, and commanded by Colonel Turner of the First Illinois. The brigade was assigned to a Provisional Division commanded by General J. C. Bates, our designation being the Second Brigade, Provisional Division.[6] As we were so widely separated from the other regiments of the division, orders and instructions mostly came to us direct from the commander of the army in Cuba, until we moved to San Juan Hill, after which they came to us generally through regular channels.

One of the several orders issued regarding the embarkation of the regiment for the north contemplated leaving behind a detail of a surgeon, a commissioned officer, and a number of men to look after the sick. Surgeon Major Farquhar intimated a willingness to remain if necessary, and when the matter was under discussion among the officers Lieutenant Hall of Company E and Lieutenant Spidel of Company F promptly volunteered for that duty. Under the changed conditions, however, that existed at the time of our embarkation, it was not necessary to leave a detail and this sacrifice was not required.

A few days after the harbor was opened to traffic by the removal of the mines placed there by the Spanish, the commissary began to make occasional issues of fresh beef, brought from the States in cold-storage vessels. Several times while we lay on Sevilla Hill, the quartermaster put in his requisition for fresh meat and secured it. Once or twice he succeeded in getting it to camp before it spoiled. But on other occasions by the time the teams reached us the odor could be detected a hundred yards away. The surgeons condemned it and it was hauled off and buried. It was found impossble to transport refrigerated meat that distance in the hot sun before it spoiled, and the effort was abandoned. When we moved up nearer the city we had fresh beef frequently.[7]

During the interim between the removal of the quarantine and our sailing for home, Captain Gyger of Company K and Lieutenant Anderson of Company E went to the hospital, from which they were transferred to the relief ship *Olivette* and sailed for Boston on the fifteenth of August, where they remained until September 12 when Lieutenant Anderson was ordered home and Captain Gyger to Washington Barracks.

Lieutenant A. T. Weybrecht was sent home sick on the first of August.

The same day that General Shafter received the order to move his army to Montauk Point, August 4, Lieutenant Colonel Dick was granted a leave of absence, and sailed home by way of New Orleans on the fifth or sixth.

Captain Feederle of Company B was taken sick about August 6 and in a few days his case was pronounced clear yellow fever, and he was sent to the yellow fever hospital across Santiago Bay. Lieutenant Schaber and Sergeant Major Reid of the 1st Battalion went to the hospital but got along fairly well and were able to join the regiment on the *Mohawk*.

A day or two before our departure for Montauk Point, a cable order was received by the commanding officer, directing him to grant an immediate discharge to Sergeant Ralph L. Spotts of Company I, and announcing the appointment of Sergeant Spotts to a captaincy in the staff department. Captain Spotts was ordered to report at once at Washington for assignment, and went on board a transport the same day. Before leaving camp he was heartily congratulated by officers and men on his good fortune.

On the morning of August 16 the following order was received:

Headquarters, V Army Corps
Santiago de Cuba, August 16, 1898

The commanding officer
Eighth Ohio Volunteer Infantry

Sir:

I am directed to say your regiment will sail on the *Mohawk* tomorrow, but should load this afternoon. Send in a report of your strength at once, officers and men, specifying strength of companies. Medical officers have been instructed to examine your command this morning. I will notify the quartermaster's department that you will need wagons.

Very respectfully,
E. J. McClernand
Assistant adjutant general

Preparations were at once begun for the movement. Dinner was ordered for eleven o'clock. Messengers were at once dispatched to Sevilla Hill and various hospitals, at which there were members of the regiment, to gather in everybody. As has already been intimated we were determined to take everybody with us who could by any means be taken on board, although it was clearly the purpose of the authorities to allow only those to embark who could pass a medical examination. There were two good reasons for this determination on the part of the officers of our regiment. First the hospital appliances and accommodations were wholly inadequate for the proper care of the sick on the island. We could take just as good care of them on shipboard for the five or six days of the voyage as they would get in the hospitals in Cuba, with the certainty of finding at Montauk excellent hospitals and everything that medical skill and a generous government and a people running over with sympathy could devise to comfort and cure them. Then we knew, too, the depressing effect it would have on the sick to leave them behind with the knowledge that they had been pronounced too ill to travel, or infected with yellow fever, while we sailed away for home. Many of them would have become at once utterly despondent and would never have lived to see home.

It began to rain early in the forenoon, the severest downpour we had experienced saving that of our first night on the island. The orders issued were to leave camp promptly at two o'clock, but when that hour arrived it was utterly impossible to move. It was four o'clock before the storm showed signs of abatement. Immediately the regiment was formed, and bidding good-by to our old tents and abandoned equipment we struck out through the mud and water for the city. Many of those who were too weak to march the entire distance were sent ahead in wagons or under the charge of comrades, who carried their kits for them. These were directed to halt at the "merry-go-round" in the suburbs and await the arrival of the main body. Just as we were entering the city, Adjutant Maynes who had gone to General Shafter's headquarters reported that while in the general's office the quartermaster general had telephoned to headquarters that the surgeons who had boarded the *Mohawk* and inspected it reported that it was unfit to transport the troops without being further cleaned, that he had instructed an officer to clean it thoroughly, and that it would not be in readiness until the next day. General Shafter at once told Adjutant Maynes to report to the colonel and say that he should remain in camp until the next day. The adjutant replied that it was then too late as the regiment had left its camp, had destroyed the stores as directed in the order to move, and was at that moment only a few squares away. The general then said to Captain Maynes that under the circumstances the only thing for us to do was to come on into the city and make the best of the situation.

The whole column was closed up, and in a compact column of fours we marched down through the narrow streets of Santiago, our colors flying, and the matchless Eighth Regiment band playing. It was really a thrilling sight. It stirred the denizens of that old city more than anything that occurred during the war. In an instant the streets were packed with a wild mob of Cubans cheering and dancing and crying. The colony of newspapermen during the evening assured the officers that the little march of the Eighth Ohio through the city had done more to impress the Cubans than any other occurrence of the occupation and that the Eighth was the only regiment up to that time that had gone through with its head up and its feathers flying. We surrounded the four sides of the "plaza" with the head in front of the governor's palace where the band played the "Star Spangled Banner," and for the first time, "Home Sweet Home." Then we resumed our march down Marina Street, the same highway over which Don Diego Velásquez galloped one November morning 380 years before to head off Mr. Hernando Cortés who had stolen a march on him while he slept and was sailing away on his voyage for the conquest of Mexico.

Halfway down to the wharf we met Major Ives, surgeon of our division, who said to the commanding officer that he was sorry he had not been able to get word to us before we broke camp, and that had he been able to do so we would have stayed in camp a day or two longer. He had just finished an inspection of the *Mohawk,* and condemned it as utterly unfit, in its present condition, to be occuped as a transport. He had reported to the corps quartermaster and that officer had ordered some subordinate to take a company of eighty Cubans, go down the bay to the vessel, and give it a thorough cleaning. It was then after six o'clock. If the stevedores worked all night it would take them until morning to clean the vessel. We were at least two miles from our old camp which we had left under water. To go back meant to land there in the mud and water long after dark, without rations, and with half the men unable to get there, scattered along the route. It was at least dry in the city, and we could get something to eat. Besides we were there in obedience to orders. The only thing left for us to do, therefore, was to go on down to the wharf and make the best of it, and we did it. We found the streets along the water front filled with artillery and a couple of battalions of infantry who had been caught just as we were. While they were waiting for instruction we took possession of one vacant wharf where a large part of the regiment was quartered; some were quartered in unoccupied portions of another wharf, and the rest made themselves comfortable on the streets, or on hay bales and oat sacks. An hour was spent in trying to find some officer who could impart some information regarding the *Mohawk,* but without success. The quartermaster general had gone down the bay three miles to the vessel on which he was quartered, and would not return until morning; his subordinates knew nothing about the situation, and there was no tug or other conveyance with which to reach him. There was nothing to do but wait.

A little commotion was created about the governor's palace that evening over the Eighth Ohio, which we found on our return home had been variously reported and not always correctly. We were charged with the shortcomings of somebody else, and a brief but highly interesting conversation ensued between

General Lawton and the commanding officer of the Eighth who defended the regiment against the charges. This is about what occurred.

About half past eight o'clock while a large number of officers, including many of the Eighth Ohio, were seated around the tables in the San Carlos Club eating supper, two officers of General Wood's staff came in and inquired for the commanding officer of the Eighth Ohio.[8] They presented General Wood's compliments and stated that the general had information that the men of the Eighth were running wild through the city, creating disturbance in saloons and on the streets, and one of them had been shot; and that General Wood desired to see Colonel Hard at his quarters immediately. Adjutant Maynes, who was present, was at once directed to detail Captain Fisher, two lieutenants, and one hundred men to patrol the city in squads and gather in all men of our regiment.

Then I proceeded to General Wood's quarters. He repeated the statement about the Ohio men, and explained the circumstances connected with the shooting. Three men, it was said, had gone into the residence of a citizen where some young ladies were heard playing on a piano, and had grossly insulted and assaulted them. The father had come to the rescue, a lot of shooting had taken place, and one of the soldiers had been badly wounded in the abdomen. It was said these men belonged to the Eighth Ohio. I explained to General Wood the measures taken to get our men back to quarters and at the same time expressed a doubt as to these disturbers being men of the Eighth. As I left the office at the close of the interview I noticed through the open door on the opposite side of the hall General Lawton sitting at a table in the center of the large room. He had just been selected to take command of the department when General Shafter should depart, and was there, evidently, getting acquainted with the situation. It occurred to me it would be the proper thing to congratulate him and bid him good-by. Acting on the impulse I stepped in, saluted, and said, "General, I brought my regiment in this afternoon to embark on the *Mohawk,* but on reaching the wharf found the steamer was not prepared. We expect to embark early in the morning and I thought I would congratulate you on your assignment and bid you good-by."

General Lawton answered courteously, and at once commenced to relate the story of the misconduct of the Ohio men, and as he proceeded he became more and more enraged until at length he was white with anger. "What in hell did you come in here at this time of night for with your regiment? Why didn't you stay in camp until your steamer was ready for you? Why don't you go and get your steamer ready? What are you up here for? Why ain't you with your regiment where you belong? What in hell is that band making so much noise for? Don't you know any better than to bring your regiment in here at this time of night to get drunk and raise hell? I've a notion to take your sword from you and put your regiment in command of somebody who has some judgment." All this without an opportunity being given for reply.

By that time I, too, was angry, and replied with a good deal of warmth, "You have asked me a whole lot of questions, general, and I'll answer them for you. I am in here with my regiment in obedience to an order from the commander of this army, Major General William R. Shafter. I have his order in my pocket, and can show it to you if I want to, but I won't do it. The reason we are not on the steamer is that the quartermaster who is in charge of the transportation has neglected to get it ready, and has gone three miles down the bay where he can't be reached. I've got twelve hundred men down here on the wharf, ordered in to embark on the *Mohawk,* and then turned loose without shelter or rations, because the steamer is not ready. I don't believe it is the men of the Eighth Ohio who are creating this disturbance. The only thing they are doing is trying to get something to eat, and they will pay for all they get. You want to know what I am up here for. I am up here with other officers of my regiment to get something to eat and we are going to stay until we get it. If you think it wise to arrest me for obeying the order to march in here this afternoon just go ahead. You'll find you've made the biggest mistake you've made since you came to Cuba."

By that time the general discovered that he had been a little too fast, and he was quick to say so. "I beg your pardon, colonel. I ought to have heard your statement perhaps before saying so much, but I have been annoyed and irritated beyond measure by the disorder this afternoon and evening. I don't want the United States Army to be disgraced by such conduct just as we are leaving after such a good record as we have established here. I hope you will help me maintain order."

I saluted, said good night, and walked out of the room in a rather unamiable frame of mind. Within an hour we learned that the men who committed the assault, and the man who was shot, belonged to the Eighth U.S. Infantry and not to the Eighth Ohio. The wounded man died before morning.

The patrol picked up a good number of our men, but they found everywhere a large number of men belonging to Regular regiments, and they also found it was these same Regulars who were having the fun and creating whatever disturbance there was, which seemed to have been greatly exaggerated.

The story of this episode is repeated here, not for the purpose of reflecting odium on General Lawton but rather to place on record a correct statement of what took place. Nobody heard the conversation but the two parties to it, unless from so great a distance that it would be indistinct. It "lasted very quick." One correspondent wrote his paper that the colonel of the Eighth wound up the defense of his regiment with a veiled threat that when he got back home he would tell the President a tale about the treatment accorded the Volunteers that would raise the dead. The fact is nothing of the kind was said or thought of. The commanding officer neither on this or any other occasion during the service ever undertook to trade upon his influence with the President—if he had any.

General Lawton was an excellent soldier. It was in everybody's mouth in Santiago that he had saved the day at El Caney. When a verbal order came to him in the midst of that fight, directing him to withdraw his forces and abandon the attack, he replied that that was too grave a step to take on a verbal order, and insisted on written instructions. When the staff officer returned with the written order it was too late—Lawton's men were then rushing the Spanish lines, and in a few moments had possession. If he had withdrawn, the history of Cuba and the United States might have been different. His subsequent services in the Philippines, and his death in battle in that far-off land, have assured him a place in history and in the hearts of his countrymen.[9]

The instant the order to embark was received, on the morning of the sixteenth, a messenger with an army wagon was sent to Major Farquhar on Sevilla Hill, and another, also with a four-mule wagon, to Dr. Carling at Major Weybrecht's old camp, with directions to these officers to bring all their men in at once and join the regiment in the embarkation. The messenger with his wagon reached Major Farquhar, and he with his whole outfit came in promptly. The orderly sent to Dr. Carling met with a mishap by which his wagon was broken down and wrecked, and he himself was unable to go forward or return because of the high waters. Nothing was heard of him until late the next afternoon. When the messenger to Dr. Carling failed to report, and nothing was heard from the doctor, another was sent out who returned and reported that he had found the camp abandoned and no traces of the men anywhere. He had missed them somewhere on the road. It was then concluded they had all been taken to the hospitals. To make sure, however, Lieutenant Hughes was sent out again toward the old camp, while Major Farquhar searched the hospitals. Neither of them found the men, but got some clues to their whereabouts. We had a great deal of anxiety about these seven or eight "lost men." Finally they drove down to the wharf, an hour before we sailed, were taken on board, and came home with us. Major Farquhar had learned that they were coming, and the departure was delayed to take them in.

Among the sick who came in from Sevilla Hill were half a dozen pretty severe cases. The examining board passed all but two of these—Privates Naftzger and Weaver of Company D. These were found to be quite ill with yellow fever. They were ordered sent to the yellow fever hospital, and the others allowed to board the steamer. Naftzger died the day after we sailed, while Weaver recovered and returned home a month or so later.[10]

VII

Aboard the *Mohawk*

At an early hour on the morning of the seventeenth the matter of embarkation was resumed. A call on Lieutenant Colonel Humphreys, corps quartermaster, developed the fact that the gang of laborers who had been engaged in cleaning the steamer had flatly refused to work at night. Nothing had been done. Summoning a steam tug we went down to the vessel to investigate and devise measures to have her properly swept and garnished—Lieutenant Colonel Humphreys, a subordinate officer of his department, the commanding officer of the Eighth, Captain Maynes, Captain Kuhns, and Surgeon Smith.

The *Mohawk* was an iron steamer, one of six of the same dimensions, belonging to the Atlantic Transport Company, and purchased at the outbreak of the war by the United States Government for transport service. She was built for and adapted to combined passenger and freight traffic, with accommodations for fity or sixty cabin passengers; the rest of her space was devoted to freight. At the time she came to Santiago she had just carried to Puerto Rico the 11th U.S. Infantry, 1,000 men and about 600 mules.[1] This was a much larger cargo than we were taking on board, as we had 1,200 men and only 15 or 20 horses. She was 520 feet long—only 40 feet less than the *St. Paul*—and 50 feet in breadth. Her depth of hold was approximately the same as the *St. Paul*. She carried no armament to occupy the space, and no freight except the luggage and ten days' rations of our regiment; whereas, it will be remembered, the *St. Paul* had six guns on her decks, carried 2,000 men, thirty days' rations for the Eighth, and an immense supply of ammunition, entrenching tools, clothing, and subsistence for Shafter's army, which weighed her down deep in the water. After going through the vessel from stem to stern and from deck to hold it was the unanimous conclusion of the officers present that we were fortunate in being assigned to so roomy and comfortable a transport. There was easily fifty percent more space at our command than there had been on the *St. Paul*.

The captain and crew were English and Scotch, one of the conditions of the sale to the United States Government being that officers and crew should remain and sail the vessel for six months. Colonel Humphreys was indignant at the captain for the indifferent manner in which he had cleaned his vessel and said picturesque things to him.

After our inspection the matter of getting it promptly and thoroughly cleaned had to be settled. Colonel Humphreys was disgusted with his gang of laborers and said that they would not work unless somebody was at hand to club them or throw them overboard. He had no officers to detail for the supervision of the work and it looked as if we might be detained another day or two. At this point Captain Maynes offered to take charge of the work if it was put into his hands, the laborers put under his orders, and he allowed to detail from the Eighth a number of officers and men to aid in making the work move off with neatness and dispatch. This was at once agreed to. Eighty men armed with hoes, shovels, and brooms were at once put to work and the vessel was scraped, swept, and scrubbed. It was not a holiday entertainment by any means, and it was three o'clock in the afternoon before Captain Maynes was able to come up to the city and announce that the *Mohawk* was ready. If we had waited for the initiative of the quartermaster's department, which was at that moment overwhelmed with difficulties like this of ours, or if we had depended on the deliberate methods of the stevedores, who were thoroughly lazy and insubordinate unless they knew they were under the eyes of an officer whose "gun" was visible on his hip, we would have been compelled to lie around the filthy, stinking wharves and streets of Santiago forty-eight hours longer or march back to our abandoned camp on San Juan Hill. Either course would have had a bad effect on the health of the men.

Only two or three days before we embarked, early one morning the First District of Columbia marched past our camp on its way to the city to take a steamer for Montauk. Our boys congregated on the side of the road and congratulated the men of the D.C. on their good fortune in "getting out," who in turn commiserated us because we were left behind. That same evening they came straggling back in squads of three or a dozen or twenty, crestfallen and mad clear through. On reaching the wharf the colonel of the D.C.'s had gone on board his transport, as required, to inspect it, and had reported to headquarters that it was "unfit" and that he would not take his men on board. Whereupon General Shafter, whose staff officers had inspected and reported the vessel in good condition, in his most suave and Chesterfieldian manner had advised the colonel that he might take his regiment and get him to a nunnery with the utmost expedition, or words to that effect; and that now the First District of Columbia would go north when he—General Shafter—got a good ready. They were one of the last regiments of V Corps to leave the island.

As soon as it was known our steamer was ready, the regiment was sent down, the last of them reaching the decks before dark, and spent the night on board. We were not ready to sail, however, as the baggage, rations, horses, and supplies were not yet all on board.

At the same time that the commanding general of the army in Cuba ordered the regiment to embark on the *Mohawk,* he directed the quartermaster to make a requisition on the post commissary for ten days' travel rations for the number of men to be transported. Army regulations provide certain kinds and quantities of subsistence for troops in camp, garrison, or when in active service in the field. These are known as field rations. When troops travel by rail or water, where they have no facilities for cooking, another kind of ration is provided, known as the travel rations. It is the ration that was issued to every soldier who was transported from Santiago to Camp Wikoff. We therefore had ten days' rations with which to subsist six days, or nearly two days' rations for each man for each day. This subsistence consists of hard bread, canned beef, canned beans, canned tomatoes, coffee, and sugar.

The balance of our supplies, the horses and luggage, were all loaded early on the morning of the eighteenth. The supply of ice furnished us was totally inadequate to meet the actual necessities of the situation. A visit to corps headquarters and a vigorous expostulation resulted in a large addition to our stock, but even that was exhausted before our voyage came to an end.

Then again about noon of the eighteenth the quartermaster of the vessel, Captain Fenton of the United States Army, met the commanding officer on the street in Santiago and made a forcible presentation of the fact that there was not enough fresh water on the steamer to guard against contingencies; that the condenser was not to be relied upon for an emergency; and that he had just escaped with a whole hide from an interview with Colonel Humphreys in which he had requested more water, with the result that the colonel had abused him and hurled harsh words at him and refused to grant his request. The captain, who was a young man, felt hurt and humiliated, as well as much worried about the supply of water, and urged the commanding officer to go to the post quartermaster and insist on a sufficient supply. His suggestion was followed, and after a brief conference with Colonel Humphreys he agreed to send down the water boat with another load; by two o'clock it was in the tanks of the *Mohawk*.

The last report was turned over to the proper staff officer at headquarters, examined and approved; the final statements of those left in hospital were handed over to the adjutant general; our sailing orders delivered to the commanding officer; and the half-dozen officers and men left to close up the business said good-by to headquarters, boarded a steam launch and dropped down to the *Mohawk*. Presently a little boat, rowed by two men, came down headed direct for us, pulled up alongside the great iron steamer, looking like a fly on an elephant's trunk; a twenty- of thirty-foot rope ladder was let down over the sides, and a wiry, husky-looking fellow, black as the ace of spades, clambered up to the deck, held a brief conference with the regimental commander and the captain of the vessel, and then took charge of the wheel. In a few moments the vessel began to move and the journey home was begun.

Among the vessels we passed as we slowly picked our way through the fleet that filled the harbor were two or three great black steamers with unpronounceable and meaningless names on their sides, loaded to the guards with sick, hungry, thinly clad, whipped Spanish soldiers, doing just what we were doing—going home. They appeared to feel just as jolly about it as our fellows did. Our band played and the boys cheered. The Spaniards answered the cheers and waved their white hats, while one enthusiastic descendant of Don Quixote or Sancho Panza climbed upon the bridge, or the pilot house, or some commanding spot, and waved the Star Spangled Banner at us as long as we could see them.

We passed the yellow fever hospital on the west side of the bay where some of our boys were then lying, among them Captain Feederle and Privates Naftzger and Weaver of Company D. On the other side we had a fine view of the residence of the British consul who had died the day before.

The *Mohawk* crept along at a snail pace, sometimes backing and filling to get through the narrow and tortuous channel. On our left were the Punta Gorda battery, the Estrella Cove and the Estrella battery, while on the right were the Smith Cay and Pilot-town that had been knocked into kindling wood by the American fleet outside.

We sailed past the hulk of the *Reina Mercedes,* with its perforated smokestacks and battered sides showing the accuracy of the Yankee gunnery, so close that one could flip a biscuit onto its deck from the *Mohawk,* and a little farther on we almost touched the sunken *Merrimac* whose chimney alone stood out of the water to mark its grave. On the right near the mouth of the harbor was the famous Socapa battery, in which one well-directed shot from the *Texas* had dismounted a six-inch gun, killed three men, and wounded six, among them the commander; and on the left, rising like Gibraltar, was the Morro, formidable looking, and in some respects formidable in fact. We could see the scars on the face of the promontory, and on the walls of the fort, where the great shells from the fleet had chipped off broad patches of stone, and hurt nobody. At the base of the rock, on the sea side, was the mouth of a cavern, which it is said is the opening to a subterranean passage, cut through solid rock, and leading up to the interior of the fort.

While waiting about the wharves on the seventeenth for the completion of the work on the *Mohawk,* the commanding officer met Mr. S. M. Jarvis of New York, vice president of the North American Trust Company, who presented a letter of introduction from a mutual friend. Mr. Jarvis, representing his company, had just taken over the business and franchises of the Spanish Cuban Bank of Santiago. During the day he introduced to the commanding officer Dr. D. T. Lainé of Philadelphia, who was anxious to go north with us on the *Mohawk*.

Dr. Lainé was a Cuban by birth, and of course an intense sympathizer with Cuba in her struggle. He was educated in the United States, a graduate of the University of Pennsylvania, spoke English fluently, and at the breaking out of the war was practicing in Philadelphia and a lecturer in the Medical College of that city. He tendered his services to the government, and after the fall of Santiago was sent to the army at that point. He was largely instrumental in organizing and maintaining the yellow fever hospital known as the Boat House Hospital. The army having returned to the States, he was ordered north and assigned to some little sawed-off transport that was about to sail with a battalion of troops. He wanted to be transferred to the *Mohawk* and appealed to Mr. Jarvis, a friend of his, for assistance, and Mr. Jarvis appealed to the regimental commander. A request was made of Lieutenant Colonel Harvard, corps surgeon, who at first flatly refused, but at length relented, and granted the order. The next day a brother of Dr. Lainé, Mr. Honoré E. Lainé, at that time a correspondent of a New York daily—the New York *Journal* in fact—requested permission to go north with us, and this was granted. Mr. Lainé was also a native of Cuba, once a strong sympathizer. Because of his Cuban proclivities he had been arrested by Weyler and imprisoned in the Havana Morro Castle.

As we passed the Morro Castle at the mouth of Santiago harbor, he was explaining its form, extent, age, etc. to a group of officers, when somebody casually asked him if he had ever been in the Morro Castle at Havana. He replied that he had; that he had been imprisoned there for a time.

"How long were you there?" he was asked.

"One year, two months, seventeen days, six hours and twenty-seven minutes!" was the reply. "I counted every minute, from the time I went in until I got out."

Standing off the mouth of the harbor was the *Yale,* waiting for something or somebody. When we reached Montauk she was there at anchor, having passed us on the way.

Then we passed out into the blue Caribbean where a first-class blow awaited us. It looked squally for a time, but before morning the wind died down, and from that time until we landed at Montauk, we had charming weather and smooth sea.

We sailed with a good many men more or less ill. Several of these developed typhoid fever before we landed. But as the orders were to take only well men aboard and to leave all sick in the hospitals at Santiago, all were classed as well.

During the voyage some dissatisfaction developed because the commissary department had not supplied us with sick rations—that is, rations adapted to the requirements of the sick. We did have a limited supply, such as is ordinarily allowed for contingencies likely to arise. But having taken these men on board the steamer as well men, if a requisition had been made for rations for sick men the response would have been prompt and emphatic: "You are not allowed to take any sick men on the transport. Your orders are to leave them all in the hospitals here. The surgeons will be directed to inspect your vessel and all sick will be brought back to shore before you can sail."

One regiment that sailed a day or two before we embarked did have just such an experience. In attempting to secure delicacies for their sick the fact was disclosed that they had taken such on their transport. An inspection was ordered and 150 or 200 men disembarked and sent back to the hospitals in Santiago. Had a requisition been made for such stores for the *Mohawk* at least 200 men who came north with us would have been left in Cuba. The men themselves were the most insistent in the desire to go home. One of the most pathetic scenes in connection with the campaign was to see some of them, weak, emaciated, and scarcely able to keep their feet, brace up and march past the inspecting surgeons, and then as soon as they were out of sight collapse utterly from the exertion. The night before he died, Corporal Tarner said to some of his comrades, "Boys, if we don't get the order to go home tomorrow morning, I shall die." And he did die only a short time before the order came.

When we were about halfway between Santiago and Montauk Point, nearly in the latitude of Charleston, South Carolina, early in the morning of August 22 occurred the death of Private Okey J. Eddy of Company E. Surgeons Smith and Wuchter who had been watching his case closely found none of the symptoms or indications of yellow fever, and only slight appearances of malaria. They were positive his ailment was not yellow fever, but were at a loss to determine what it was. Dr. Lainé examined the patient and agreed with our surgeons both in their diagnosis and treatment. If on our arrival at Montauk, our surgeon should certify that Private Eddy died August 22, cause of death unknown, the local health authorities would at once suspect that he had died of yellow fever and we were concealing the fact, or that our surgeons were not able to judge whether it was the fever or not. We would then become suspects and be subjected to all the rigid annoyances of quarantine. A post-mortem examination was therefore resolved upon to determine just what was the disorder of which Eddy died. Dr. Lainé took charge of the autopsy and was assisted by Surgeons Smith and Wuchter, the former of whom took the notes of the examination. The result was that all the organs were found in perfect condition except the liver, and that was only slightly disordered. The cause of death was found to be intussusception of the intestines—that is, the reception of the upper portion of the small intestine into the lower.

At the rate at which we were then steaming it was calculated that it would take us two and a half or three days to reach our destination. It was impossible and unwise to preserve the body so long as that. Preparations were therefore made at once to give him a sailor's burial. The men of the *Mohawk* took charge of the arrangements. The body was tightly sewed up in a sack with a fifty-pound weight at the feet. It was placed on a gangplank on an upper deck, the inner end slightly elevated so that it dipped toward the sea. An American flag covered the body. Two or three sailors stood on either side, near the head, ready at the proper moment to raise the plank and allow the dead soldier to slide into the water. Chaplain Campbell, and the officers of the dead soldier's company, together with the regimental officers, gathered around the head, while as many of his comrades as could do so stood around on the decks and filled the rigging. The chaplain read the service for the burial of the dead from the prayer book. As the ceremonies began the engines slowed up, and just before the end the great steamer came to a dead standstill. As the chaplain pronounced the momentous sentence, "We therefore commit his body to the deep," the sailors raised the end of the gangplank, the flag was quickly removed, the body shot into the sea, and those on the gunwales could see it rapidly sink through the blue waters, and all that was mortal of the brave soldier was lost to human sight, to be restored only when the sea shall give up her dead. Then the wheels began to move, the steamer shot ahead, and the sad incident was closed.

The government transport service, it must be admitted, was at this stage of the game somewhat defective. The *Mohawk* was one of the first-class vessels then in the service. She was as good as any, and better than most of them. The sinks were unwisely placed, and poorly constructed. The sleeping bunks were contracted, and crowded, and the ventilation was something awful—or rather the lack of ventilation. There was a good deal of deck space, and on this several hundred men slept nightly, which was a great relief to the situation. Provision was made by the government for furnishing the men with hot coffee, but aside from the appliances for cooking for the crew, and the limited number of passengers the vessel was fitted to carry, there were no facilities whatever provided for supplying the men with any kind of cooked rations. This was true of all transports at that time, the authorities, as already explained, intending the troops to subsist for the brief period on the prepared travel ration.

The first day out from Santiago the quartermaster undertook, with the steward of the steamer, to devise some means to furnish the troops with hot soup once a day. A couple of discarded copper kettles were found among the ship's supplies, both of which needed patching and repairing before they would hold water. One was made ready by the next morning, and as much soup as it would hold was prepared and served to each man—rather a small portion it must be admitted, but it was just that much more than the government had provided for us. Some of the men were dissatisfied with the supply of soup furnished them and gave vent to their feelings in what is commonly denominated a kick. The second kettle was completed the next day and thereafter 120 gallons of soup was issued to the men once each day. The quartermaster also purchased of the ship's steward all the rice and barley he could spare, and added these to the tomatoes we had among our rations to give more substance to the soup. Major Vollrath suggested that the officers forego the rice, peas, and barley, and any other vegetables served to them by the steward and laid the proposition before him. The steward, of course, said that he would carry out such instructions, but added, and demonstrated clearly, that all the vegetables of that character that he would serve to the officers' mess during the remainder of the trip would scarcely be noticeable in a simple issue of 120 gallons of soup. The idea was therefore abandoned.

In addition to the soup mentioned above as issued to the men, Captain Kuhns each day during the trip made in the steamer's kitchen from six to eight gallons of fine soup to be issued to the more seriously ill, turning it over to the surgeons and hospital stewards for proper distribution.[2]

The travel ration constitutes a menu of which one is apt to tire in a short time. It will undoubtedly sustain life a great many years, and it would be difficult to starve on it. But an uninterrupted diet of canned boiled beef, canned baked beans, and canned tomatoes soon becomes exceedingly monotonous. The men on the *Mohawk,* sick and debilitated, many of them, soon turned against the ration, and then when some of the hard bread, when the boxes were opened, was found to be wormy, they grumbled. When any hard bread, thus infested, was issued, it was ordered withdrawn, and good bread, of which there was an abundance, was issued in its stead.[3]

All these annoyances caused an occasional unpleasantness. For instance, it was a standing order every morning at guard mounting to detail one hundred men to police the quarters, that is, to clean and sweep up the portions of the vessel occupied by the troops. This was done in the interest of simple cleanliness and health, and generally took only twenty or thirty minutes. One morning after guard mounting the officer of the day reported that three of the detail, members of one company, refused to do duty, alleging that they had nothing to eat. The officer was directed to bring them to headquarters, where the gravity of the offense was pointed out to them. They asserted that they had had no breakfast, except a few spoonfuls of coffee and a hardtack. They were assured that they were entitled to a full day's rations, and if they did not receive them somebody was derelict. The first sergeant of their company, Sergeant W. F. Hanley, was sent for. Their statement was repeated to him, and on their reiterating it he assured them in the most vigorous language a soldier can command that the statements they had made were utterly at variance with the facts in the case. The men still refusing to obey orders there was presented a simple proposition of discipline. They were sent to the brig on bread and water, and at the end of thirty-six hours expressed themselves as willing to do any duty required by them. This was the only case of flat insubordination that occurred during the service.

VIII

Montauk Point

The evening after we cast anchor off Montauk Point, August 24, Private John Roos of Company B died on board the *Mohawk*. His body was taken on shore on the morning of the twenty-fifth and for the same reasons that prevailed in the case of Private Eddy an autopsy was held on the wharf by two surgeons of the local board of health, which developed the fact that he had malarial fever and that death was caused by organic disease of the heart and kidneys. In addition to demonstrating beyond question that we had no yellow fever, the post-mortem examinations of Privates Eddy and Roos were fortunate for another reason. On the day of our landing, August 26, a highly sensational dispatch was sent out from Montauk to Cincinnati, Cleveland, and Pittsburgh papers telling a harrowing tale of deaths by starvation on the *Mohawk*. The information purported to be given by "a soldier who came ashore from the *Mohawk* yesterday—he is not a member of the 'President's Own' as the Eighth Ohio is known." It stated that "the rations were wholly inadequate and the sick fairly starved. Roos and Eddy were victims of starvation as surely as I stand here." This was published by Ohio papers and by New York City papers with startling headlines like this:

EIGHTH OHIO BOYS STARVED TO DEATH
TERRIBLE SUFFERINGS OF BRAVE OHIO VOLUNTEERS

in type large enough for one of Van Amburg's circus posters. As a matter of fact there was no "soldier . . . not a member of the 'President's Own' " on the *Mohawk*. He was the creature of some enterprising newspaper correspondent's vivid imagination.[1]

Over against the alleged story of this phantom soldier, "not a member of the 'President's Own,' " set the official statements of the surgeons who attended Eddy and Roos in their sickness and were with them at death, and the sensation like many another one constructed about this time is shown to have been "baseless as the fabric of a vision."

Soon after we dropped anchor in the bay off Montauk a tug came out from the wharf and Dr. Magruder, the local health officer, accompanied by two or three other medical officers, came on board. They called for the commanding officer and the surgeon of the regiment, received a report, and made an inspection of the men. After an hour spent in the inspection Dr. Magruder advised the commanding officer that he found the regiment in better physical condition than any other that he had examined, and that he would report to the commander at Camp Wikoff that there were no reasons why we should not disembark at once. He commended in highly complimentary terms the foresight shown in having an autopsy held on the body of the soldier who died at sea. He said this was the first autopsy that had been held on any transport carrying troops from Cuba to Montauk Point, and that had the same course been pursued by the commander of every body of soldiers coming from Santiago it would have simplified matters for him and been much better for the troops. The next morning he readily acceded to the request to make a post-mortem examination of the body of Private Roos, and designated two of his assistants to perform the operation. In his report Dr. Magruder said, "Four or five cases of sickness in the Eighth are serious, though not dangerous. On the whole I have not boarded a transport coming from Cuba with the health of the troops in a better shape."

Notwithstanding this statement by the officer best qualified of any on Long Island to know the situation, the yellow journals of New York and their imitators elsewhere continued for a number of days to publish startling stories with enormous headlines about the awful sickness and suffering and starvation on the *Mohawk*.

A number of the officers were sick on the *Mohawk,* some of them seriously so. Of the medical staff Surgeons Farquhar and Wuchter, and Hospital Steward Struggles were more or less ill; and Captain Lee, Lieutenant Swingly, Lieutenant Taylor, Lieutenant Bolich, Captain Willis, Lieutenant Hard, Captain Marquis, and Lieutenant Burson had to give up the fight and go to their bunks. Farquhar, Willis, Taylor, and Struggles were the most serious, and at least three of them were at once suspected of having typhoid fever—Willis, Taylor, and Struggles.

In accordance with the arrangements made the day before, early in the morning of the twenty-fifth a small steamer, evidently one of the many excursion boats running out of New York, pulled up alongside the *Mohawk* to take our sick men ashore. Two of the surgeons were stationed at the end of the gangplank leading down to the lighter with instructions to allow none but the sick to pass. A detail of fifty men under command of Captain Critchfield was assigned to the duty of helping the men onto the lighter. They also went ashore with them, put them into the ambulances, took charge of their luggage, and went with them to the detention camp hospital. The worst patients were first taken down. These had to be carried on cots or stretchers and handled carefully. Many of them were so weak that it took one or two comrades to support them and conduct them across the constantly moving gangplank. Here again were displayed some of the noblest traits of character. Beneath the greasy, mud-stained khaki of these men of the Eighth were hearts as big as haystacks. When a pale, tottering, skeleton-like fellow walked onto the gangplank, hesitating at the journey across that uncertain bridge, a great big, bearded, rough-looking comrade called to him, "Here, old man! I'll carry you over." And taking him in his arms like a child, he carried him safely over and set him down on the deck of the hospital boat, as gently as a mother with her first-born babe. There was a constant stream of homely yet gentle and encouraging speech addressed to the sick, "Come on, pard! Put your arm around my neck and I'll take care of you!" "Brace up, old fellow! Right over there's God's country!" "You're all right, Charlie! You'll be well in a day or two!" "Here! You old Cubian! Give me your traps!" And to one young fellow, half delirious with fever, who hesitated about letting go of his rifle while he was carried over lest it should be lost, "Damn the gun! It's you we want! The gun ain't sick and you are!"

The transfer was not wholly destitute of ludicrous elements. One man who was probably so sick that he did not know what he was doing surrendered his roll, his haversack, and cartridge belt, and canteen and rifle, to his guides, but hung like grim death to a little wooden cage with a parrot in it, and utterly refused to give it up even for the moment. At one time a laugh was raised at a stout healthy man who undertook to pass himself over as a sick man. He was recognized by somebody who knew he was not sick, and dodged back amid shouts of laughter at the failure of his game.

When this work was finished it was found that the score footed up 294 sick taken on the transfer steamer. Not all of these were bad cases. More than half of them perhaps were able to go over with little assistance.

We at once cut loose from the troopship and steamed in to the wharf some two miles away, inside the lines of the detention camp. As we pulled up an elderly officer came down the dock to the vessel and introduced himself to the commanding officer as Colonel Hecker. He represented Secretary Alger and was there to do anything or everything for us that needed to be done. He stated that the hospital appliances and appointments were splendid and that there were many trained nurses on the ground and more coming. The government was supplying unlimited quantities of everything to eat and of the best that could be had in the market—fresh bread, eggs, milk, meat, vegetables, and fruit. When asked if some of these could be had for our men on the *Mohawk* he replied, "You shall have what you want."

A hurried calculation was made and in a couple of hours a wagon came down with eighteen ten-gallon cans of fresh milk, enough for nearly a quart for each man. A little later a big army wagon unloaded barrels and crates containing eight hundred loaves of fresh bread and a thousand pounds of fresh beef. These were all put on the little steamer and when we went back, about five o'clock, turned over to the tender mercies of the eight hundred men on the *Mohawk*.

The men were unloaded and sent out to the hospital as rapidly as possible but it was a slow operation. The number of ambulances was limited, the hospitals a mile or a mile and a half away, and the roads heavy with sand. It was nearly five o'clock when the last ambulance had started.

During the day, while on shore, those of us who expected to go back to the *Mohawk* were not allowed to pass the guards along the line of the camp, and those in the camp could not pass onto the wharf unless they intended to remain, the only exception to this order being in the case of officers whose duties required them to come onto our side of the line. A number of friends and relatives of the men of the Eighth from Ohio came down to the guard line and inquired about their people. Among these were Mr. Brosius of Alliance, the father of Lieutenant Brosius, and Mr. Birk of Bucyrus, the father of Lieutenant Birk. A touching occurrence was connected with Mr. Birk's visit. When these two gentlemen came up to the guard the commanding officer, seeing them, went over and met them. Mr. Birk asked for his son, and was told that he was well and was at that moment not far away. He wanted to know if the lieutenant had heard of his mother's death, and was informed that he certainly had not. It fell upon his father to greet his son on his return with the sad news that his mother was dead and buried.

The excitement and anxiety created among our friends at home by the sensational newspapers about this time was made apparent on this day. While supervising the transfer of the sick the commanding officer received and answered between 140 and 150 telegrams inquiring as to the health or condition or whereabouts of some men of the Eighth. It was a source of gratification that with very few exceptions the answers to these telegrams relieved somebody's anxiety.

Next day, the twenty-sixth, toward noon, the *Mohawk* steamed in, tied up beside a big wharf, and the disembarkation began, in regular order. Lieutenant

Colonel Dick, who had been at home some weeks, met us. An association of New York ladies had stationed a booth at the end of the wharf, and as the companies marched past every man was given a cup of cool milk and a sandwich with genuine, unadulterated butter. This was a most sensible lunch, hurt nobody, and did everybody good. In the bustle and hustle of getting the regiment out the commanding officer could not get the names of the women or the association, but whoever they were, at least eight hundred Buckeye boys thought they were angels.

While the troops were debarking, Secretary Alger drove in the lines, and inquired for the commanding officer. In a few moments' conversation he stated that he had just come from the president who had sent by him a message of love to the boys of the Eighth. He authorized the commander to deliver this message to the men and to say that the regiment would be placed in the detention camp for a few days until all danger of infection was past, and then after a few days in camp to recuperate and get ready we would be furloughed for sixty days, at the expiration of which period if our services were further required we would be ordered to camp; if not we would be mustered out of the service. The matter of the gratuitous issue of clothing, made at Santiago but not issued by the quartermaster, and held in boxes on the *Mohawk,* having been suggested, the secretary said, "Let the boys wear their old, greasy uniforms home; they are honorable; if you go into the service again you will want new clothing; if you don't go back into the service, they will not want the new uniforms; and the government will give them the money value in lieu of the clothing." The suggestion was adopted, and at the muster-out every enlisted man received between nineteen and twenty dollars extra pay.

As soon as the men were all off the steamer the regiment was formed and marched out to the detention camp. At the top of the first hill we climbed, the representatives of some tobacco house gave each man as he passed a pipe and a package of tobacco. The last thing we got before sailing for Cuba was—tobacco; and the first thing we found on returning was—tobacco. The 1st Battalion was halted on an elevation with just tents enough to accommodate its numbers, and the 2nd and 3rd Battalions with headquarters were assigned to another plateau a quarter of a mile farther on and near the hospitals. Here we spent our first night and the first three or four days of our life in Camp Wikoff.

IX

Epilogue

Colonel Hard ended his "Story of the Eighth" with arrival at Camp Wikoff, and it is necessary to give some account of how the regiment fared in its new camp and then went back to Ohio and was mustered out.

In the first days at Wikoff, Hard had his hands full explaining to reporters what really had happened on the *Mohawk*. Probably the fault lay mainly with the reporters. It was a time of shameless reportorial invention; some of the reporters were nothing less than novelists. Consider the following newspaper dispatch about the Eighth's bugler, reciting the camaraderie of the regiment while at sea. Allegedly the *Mohawk*'s engine room was shorthanded, without enough stokers to fire both boilers:

> Among the typhoid patients the most serious was that of little Jimmie Fulton, the boy bugler of the regiment. Jimmie is only fifteen, and his exposure in the sheds of Santiago had given his case a turn for the worse. Professor Lainé, of Philadelphia, who is an expert on fever cases, and who happened to be on board, was called in and did all in his power for the little bugler, but there was no improvement, and the doctor had to confess that his chances were hourly becoming worse, and that his only hope was to keep the boy alive until Montauk was reached, where it was hoped the proper nourishment could be secured and his life saved. Fulton is a member of Company A, of Bucyrus, and his comrades heard with sorrow the discouraging report of the doctor; but they were determined to do their best to defeat the grim monster death, and calling a committee together they waited upon the captain and volunteered to furnish men enough to work in the stokehole and fire the other boiler. The offer was accepted, and sick though they were the men took turns of four hours each in shoveling coal to the firemen. It was literally a race with death, and the lagging ship was speeded on to where help was hoped for. The little bugler lived to land, and may yet pull through.[1]

Colonel Hard and staff on pier in New York, sailing day for Cuba. (Library of Congress stereograph collection.)

Boarding the USS *St. Paul*. (Frank Klein, The Bookseller, Akron, Ohio.)

On deck aboard the USS *St. Paul*. (Ames Papers, Smith College.)

Unloading at Siboney, Cuba, July 1898. (Ames Papers, Smith College.)

Army mule teams haul gear to camp.

Pack train loaded with hardtack.

Camp of the Eighth Ohio, Cuba.

Horse-drawn ambulance which served the regiment.

Cemetery in Cuba.

Maj. Gen. "Fighting Joe" Wheeler, at the surrender in Santiago. Gen. Shafter, in pith helmet, has his back to the camera. (Ames Papers, Smith College.)

San Carlos Club, where the "patriotic gentlemen of Cuba . . . spend much of their time." (Ames Papers, Smith College.)

Loading horses on the USS *Mohawk*.

Burial at sea while en route to the States.

Weary men of the Eighth Ohio return from Cuba, older by years in a few short weeks. (The Western Reserve Historical Society.)

Lining up for pay, Montauk Point, Long Island.

This specially constructed barracks in Wooster housed the Eighth Ohio during their final days of military service. (The Western Reserve Historical Society.)

Colonel Hard spent his later years in Wooster, where he wrote his account of the Eighth Ohio. (*History of Wayne County, Ohio*.)

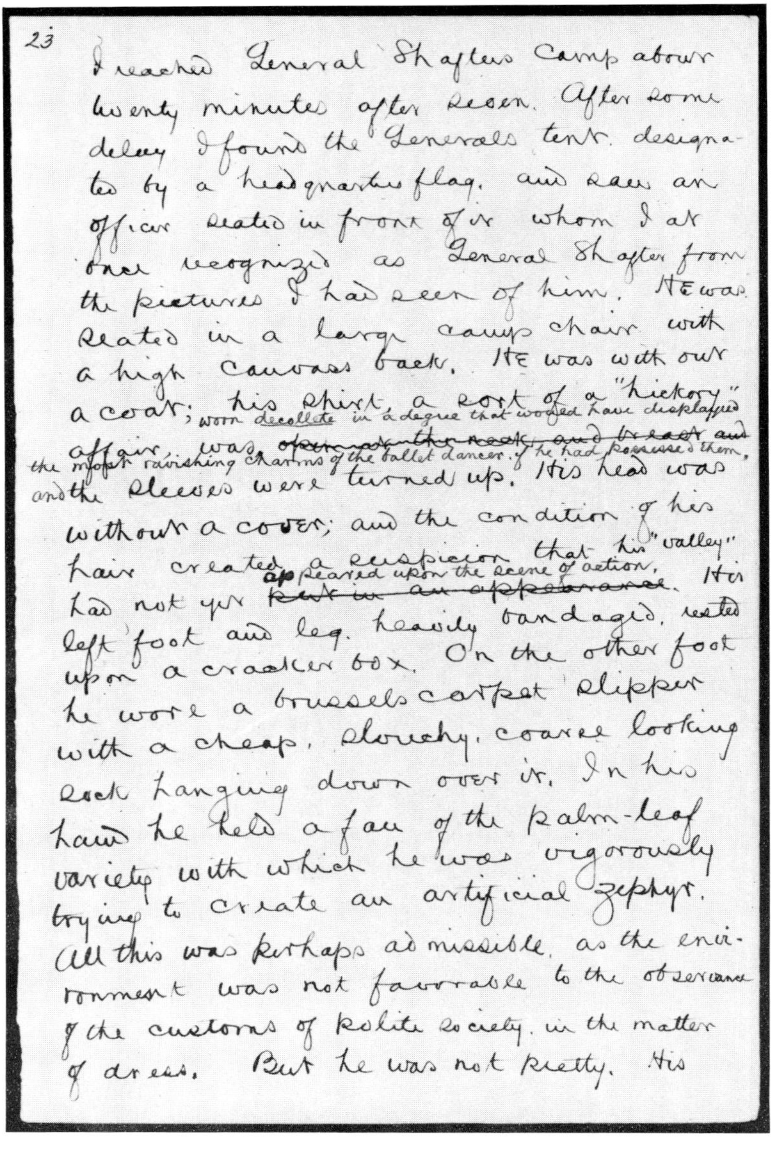

23

I reached General Shafters Camp about twenty minutes after seven. After some delay I found the Generals tent designated by a headquarters flag, and saw an officer seated in front of it whom I at once recognized as General Shafter from the pictures I had seen of him. He was seated in a large camp chair with a high canvass back. He was with out a coat; his shirt, a sort of a "hickory" affair, was ~~open at the neck, and breast and~~ worn decollete in a degree that would have displayed the most ravishing charms of the ballet dancer, if he had possessed them, and the sleeves were turned up. His head was without a cover; and the condition of his hair created a suspicion that his "valley" had not yet ~~put in an appearance~~ appeared upon the scene of action. His left foot and leg, heavily bandaged, rested upon a cracker box. On the other foot he wore a brussels carpet slipper with a cheap, slouchy, coarse looking sock hanging down over it. In his hand he held a fan of the palm-leaf variety with which he was vigorously trying to create an artificial zephyr. All this was perhaps admissible, as the environment was not favorable to the observance of the customs of polite society, in the matter of dress. But he was not pretty. His

Manuscript copy of Curtis Hard's account of the Eighth's experiences in the Spanish-American War. (The Western Reserve Historical Society.)

But then in explaining the Eighth's troubles Hard did not put his best foot forward. Reporters tended to believe that the voyage was an almost unending testimony to the colonel's incompetence. They fastened upon the Eighth's weary appearance at Montauk, including the deaths of two men aboard ship, and also on stories of starvation. Hard snappishly explained both problems. The root cause of the Eighth's troubles, the fever, he said, was the result of misbehavior. He blamed two or three members of Company D, the Wooster company, who during the Cuban campaign betrayed every one of their fellows. They violated all rules of military law by running company pickets and entering the city of Santiago—this when the company was in isolation, preparing for reassignment to Puerto Rico. "They brought the fever back with them and it spread all over the camp. For this kind of work I reduced several noncommissioned officers to the ranks and now I see these fellows are trying to square themselves in the eyes of the people by charging me with mismanagement. . . ."[2]

As for the stories of starvation, the colonel contended that at certain stages of fever, malaria, and typhoid, men acquired an abnormal appetite, and had to be kept away from heavy food. While in their hungry state, he said, they would tell marvelous tales about being starved—nothing to eat for days. Moreover, as soon as they got to Wikoff they had misbehaved and ate too much. "As soon as those fellows began to get better," he said, warming to the subject, "they would get out and gorge themselves with everything they could get their hands on and next day would have a relapse of the fever. They were overfed when they should have had but very little. . . ." He deplored the well-meaning efforts of the home folks, who sent soldiers delicacies instead of letting them eat the light fare that was best for them: it was "these boxes from home" that did the mischief.[3]

Before the regiment left Montauk there was a visit by President McKinley, during which the president inspected the entire camp for five hours, in the company of Secretary Alger and General Wheeler. The president made everyone feel better. McKinley greeted Colonel Roosevelt and the Rough Riders, and visited General Shafter in his tent; the general was recovering from his illness during the campaign and unable to go to the president. Before several regiments McKinley spoke briefly, remarking that "your personal bravery, never before excelled anywhere, has won the admiration of your fellow citizens and the genuine respect of all mankind."[4] After luncheon a photographer made a group picture of the president, Alger, Wheeler, and Colonel Hard.

When the Eighth prepared to depart, September 6, confusion arose momentarily over transportation. Secretary Alger had arranged for the Eighth to entrain for Columbus. President McKinley suggested Cleveland, which would make it easier to drop off the men at their various towns. Men were to have sixty-day furloughs, and reassemble in Wooster for mustering out. The president instructed Alger to work out details, but the secretary failed to get the new orders to the depot quartermaster in New York. Just when the regiment was preparing to leave camp in twenty cars, at 8:00 A.M., a telegram from the quartermaster related that he had no orders and did not know what he would do with a thousand men when they arrived in Long Island City. Hard informed Shafter of the hitch and a lively telegraphic exchange followed between the choleric general and the quartermaster, who was only a colonel. The train pulled out several hours later.

From that point onward, however, the trip home went without incident. The three sections of the regiment—it required three, including a section of freight cars for supplies and equipment—drew into the Buffalo depot on the evening of September 7, and passed through Erie early the next morning. At Erie the men were heartily cheered, and even though the hour was late the Soldiers' Relief Association was ready with a hearty meal of sandwiches and coffee for the soldiers who were well, chicken broth and beef tea for those who were ill. The trains arrived in Cleveland around 3:00 A.M., and men remained aboard until daylight, when they were served breakfast in the depot and greeted by a large crowd of friends. During the layover in Cleveland reporters swarmed among the men, picking up what information they could. A story circulated that one of the boys from the Mansfield company had married a Cuban girl while in that country. His comrades would not tell his name. The man had not brought the bride along, for the marriage service was in the Cuban language and the soldier husband could not understand it.[5] Souvenir hunters were in the station, and one man showed a piece of bark removed from the tree under which the surrender of Santiago took place. Many Mauser bullets were in evidence, and soldiers said they had received as high as $2.50 for them in New York.

From Cleveland the men went their separate ways, to spend furloughs at home.

During the Eighth's period of leave the citizens of Wooster prepared to receive the regiment for the mustering out. The little town of six thousand souls, in the rolling hills of central Ohio—spread along a picturesque valley and up the side of a long hill, with the buildings of Wooster College, a Presbyterian institution, rising halfway—found the enterprise of providing for the regiment a daunting experience, for how would it deal with nearly a thousand young men? A subscription was raised, to the sum of one thousand dollars, and a barracks erected on the lot adjoining the armory: 40 feet wide, 180 feet long, 12 feet high at the eaves and 20 at the peak. Bunks were four by six and one-half feet and tiers ran north and south. The barracks required

75,000 feet of lumber, six carloads weighing seven and one-half tons, and carpenters used three tons of nails. They put up the building in record time. Had a single carpenter done the work it would have taken 150 days.

Meanwhile, an abandoned shutter factory, a big, barnlike place, was converted into a dining room. The contract was given to J. N. Grant, who was to act as superintendent and engage fifteen assistants in the kitchen and fifteen waiters.

The Eighth regiment came in on Thursday, November 10, by various conveyances—Company D was already there, and men of the other companies arrived by horseback, buggy, and train. As it turned out, they spent eleven days in Wooster, waiting until the army paymaster from Columbus could bring in money for the payroll—a messenger from the Adams Express Company was reported to have brought in $100,000 in cold cash—and make other necessary arrangements.

Wooster's preparations for the regiment proved sufficient. The barracks seems to have worked out all right, although it was nothing palatial. Various of Wooster's citizens contributed cloth ticks, which were filled with straw. The men looked upon their crude quarters as temporary, and endured it, although it may have inspired some of them to "roughhousing," toward the end of the stay, when they helped the local citizenry tear down the structure. Only one open testimony against the barracks was made. Corporal William R. McCord of Company E wrote to the *East Liverpool Crisis* and his letter, alas, was rerun in the *Wooster Daily Republican*. He said that thirty boys of Company E had obtained medical certificates relating that their health would not permit them to stay in the barracks. They had engaged comfortable rooms about town for $1.50 per week, "and the soldier, stretching himself on a nice, clean sheet, once more feels as though he were a civilized creature."[6] As for the food, McCord said it was all right, even good, but the potatoes nearly always were cold when the boys sat down to the table. Another testimony, by an unnamed correspondent of the *Canton News-Democrat,* reprinted in the *Wooster Evening Journal,* related that after a while the contractor began to even up for the good meals he had served during the first two or three days.[7]

Experiences otherwise in Wooster during this final part of the regiment's military service varied with rank and, among the common soldiers, ingenuity. Newspapers carried accounts of a dance at Miller's Hall, with officers present in the company of ladies, a good time from 8:30 P.M. until midnight, and music furnished by the Eighth's band. Colonel Hard received officers and wives at his home on Beall Avenue. The men made out as best they could. Corporal McCord, an ingenious fellow, asserted that the Eighth "owned" Wooster, and told of soldiers strolling with "dormitory girls" of the college, dining at the residence known as Hoover Cottage by virture of "some fair student's hospitality." But a correspondent of a Canton paper said Wooster was about the worst place the men had ever gotten into. Even McCord admitted there were too many men for local entertainment: "A thousand fellows all looking for a good time at once in the town of Wooster. Imagine!" He heard of a man from Company E who was more thoroughly homesick in Wooster than during the regiment's entire stay in Cuba.

The men whiled away time, with two roll calls a day and dress parade in the square during afternoons. On Sunday, November 20, bandmaster Palmer brought extra instrumentalists from Akron and gave a sacred concert, which took some of the drag off the occasion.

A few troublemakers seem to have been about. Men went around town wearing buttons on their tunics bearing the legend, "Remember the *Mohawk*." A reporter heard that the life of Colonel Hard was threatened. A group of men may have gathered outside the Archer House saying they were quite anxious to meet Adjutant Maynes.

The regiment at last was paid off on Monday, November 21, with something over a hundred dollars for each man. Word had it that trouble was anticipated. Railroad police were brought in and Company D, the Wooster company, was armed. "There was some hurry in getting the boys away from the Wayne County capital," the *Canton News-Dispatch* reported, "but that just suited the soldiers. They wanted Wooster off their visiting list." That evening a special train was run over the Pennsylvania Railroad for Canton and Alliance. "Six coaches and a baggage car made up the train, which was loaded as were several of the occupants."[8]

The Eighth departed, its reputation in Wooster perhaps a bit tarnished. According to one newspaper, whose reporter was of philosophic bent, "Volunteer military bodies in time of war are necessary and expedient engines of struggle, doing their duty with courage and spirit, and asking for no reward save the plaudits of an admiring people. Peace makes of them breeding places of discontent, devilry, and leveling agencies of military pride and dignity."[9]

In subsequent years the experiences of mustering and going to Cuba, and the campaign and return to the United States, do not seem to have affected the members of the regiment in any dramatic way, such as persuading them that their lives as they had led them in the past were no longer sufficient and therefore inspiring them to push upward toward achievement of some remarkable sort. None of the enlisted men of the Eighth acquired any later prominence. Nor did the officers. Colonel Hard lived on for nearly twenty years, working faithfully as cashier of the Wooster National Bank. When he journeyed outside of Wooster he received little recognition as a businessman; his light did not shine beyond his hometown. Lieutenant Colonel Dick already had displayed ambition, well before the outbreak of the war, by obtaining appointment as secretary of the Republican National Committee. After the surrender of Santiago he had left for Washington ahead of his regiment, sent by General Shafter on a mission to President McKinley for the purpose of getting the troops out of Cuba.[10] Within weeks of the war's end he arranged for himself an appointment as major general in the Ohio National Guard. That autumn he secured a seat in the House of Representatives for the Nineteenth Ohio District, after the incumbent suddenly died. When Mark Hanna died in 1904, Dick was appointed to his Senate seat, winning it in his own right in November that year. Then he failed of reelection in 1910, and slipped into obscurity—a figure who, so an observer in Akron remarked upon his death in 1945, had been for many years a participant in local Fourth of July parades but otherwise was hardly known, even in the city in which he lived.

Still, whatever the lives of its members, the Eighth Ohio's place in history was considerable. The regiment's appearance off Santiago shortly before the fall of the city to Shafter's forces, as Consul Ramsden wrote, had given one more testimony to the Spanish defenders of the overwhelming force with which the United States in 1898 was willing to settle the Cuban revolution in favor of Cuban freedom and the retirement of Spain from the New World. Such testimony apprised other nations that American power was no longer a provincial force, to be exercised only for the Western Hemisphere, but would be a makeweight (to use the eighteenth-century word of John Adams) in the relations of the countries of Europe. Twenty years after 1898 the U.S. Army was in northern France fighting the divisions of Imperial Germany, helping to bring victory to the Western Allies. It was a mostly civilian army but much more carefully organized, with two million troops in forty-two huge divisions—each containing more men than Shafter had in Cuba. The Eighth's work in 1898 also looked to the tasks of later years, to World War II and the cold war. The men of the Eighth carried single-shot Springfield rifles, weapons a light year removed from the nuclear warheads and missiles of our time. The connection nonetheless is clear.

Appendix 1

Following is an account of the memorial service for the dead of the Eighth Ohio, held on the public square in Wooster, Nov. 16, 1898. Source: *Wooster Daily Republican*, Nov. 17.

Providence in permitting in the middle of November weather for an outdoor meeting in memory of her soldier dead, certainly smiled upon the Eighth Ohio regiment, for no house could have held the multitude that thronged the public square yesterday afternoon. It was fitting that the first use of the handsome bandstand and rostrum for public speaking should be in honor of the departed heroes for humanity of our home regiment in the American war to carry freedom to the people oppressed by Spain for centuries. The exercises, too, were appropriate to the occasion, in their simplicity and earnestness. Conducted by the regimental officers, with music by the Eighth Regiment band, all the speakers were field officers of the regiment except the Reverend Dr. H. L. Wiles, of Mansfield, who claimed the right to call them "comrade," having, when Lutheran pastor in Wooster, belonged to Company D. The invocation was by a pastor with two sons in Company D, and the benediction was pronounced with a touching prayer by the father of one of the fallen, Hospital Steward Willis Struggles. It was a remarkable and notable gathering that assembled. As far as speakers could be heard (in fact farther than that, because of needless noise in and about the crowd), men, women, and children crowded together as close as they could stand, every rank represented, the soldier beside the citizen, and all intent with interest, unusual in so great a multitude. Nothing more clearly shows the size of this assembly than that the number of soldiers' hats in the throng, although marking almost the full membership of the regiment, bore such a small proportion to the entire throng. In the great company, too, were representatives of all the towns interested, particularly friends of the men commemorated. The music by the band was appropriate and impressive and the exercises throughout were marked by military promptness that added to their effectiveness.

In fact, taking it altogether, it was an occasion honorable to Wooster and memorable in the annals of the city and the regiment.

At the appointed hour the Eighth Regiment band and officers and others to occupy the stand were there, and the delay was not theirs. When chairs were ready, the band played the "Intermezzo Sinfonico" from Mascagni's "Cavalleria Rusticana." Col. Hard presiding, stated the object of assembling. Since 1,326 men of northern Ohio seven months ago in the full vigor of youth took their lives in their hands and went forth to war, risking many climes, enduring hardships, seventy-two giving up their lives for humanity, many others are filled with the seeds of disease and will never recover. All gave their lives to their country. They met an enemy whose aim was more certain, his shafts more deadly, than any Spanish foe. The hospital tents in Cuba could tell of heroic suffering, patient endurance, far surpassing any valor in the exhilaration of battle. These men are heroes as truly as those of the battlefield, and we are here today to pay our tribute of respect.

Reverend S. M. Glenn's prayer was earnest and brief. It invoked blessings upon the bereaved friends, upon the regiment, the nation, and the cause. It asked God to grant peace and prosperity, and that the people may recognize all "as from Thy hand." God bless our enemies, give them through this greater prosperity and enlightenment. The band played "Magnolia Serenade," by Jean M. Missonid, with cornet solo by Band-master W. R. Palmer.

Maj. Frederick C. Bryan, of Akron, commander of 2nd Battalion, was called to speak first. The names of the heroes we honor are written on the record of the regiment, are engraved on our hearts, enshrined in the archives of the God of battles. They fell as brave men in the line of duty. No man can claim greater glory than these, that he died for his country. These men who were hurried to Cuba to reinforce the V Corps before Santiago are as truly entitled to share in its glory as though they had been on the battle line. We do not believe they fell in vain. Without great sacrifice, as of this regiment, no great good can be gained. God sifted Europe for the seed to plant this Republic that has made the world better. We believe God has a new mission for our country. It will not do to be too selfish, to keep this higher civilization to ourselves. God has enlarged our borders to bring new blessings to the world with our new duties. No war with higher ambitions, nobler purpose was ever known. No ignoble ambition, materialist selfishness, should hold us. We must carry the flag of liberty, of education, to these islands that have come to us. Then if we do our duty, these lives will not have been given in vain; their proudest memorial will be Paul's noble words: they have fought the good fight, they have kept the faith.

Maj. Edward Vollrath, of Bucyrus, commanding 1st Battalion, contrasted eloquently the appearance of the men as they marched through Wooster streets on their way to the front, the events at Bushnell and Alger and in Cuba, with the present. There never was a regiment in the volunteer service in better condition and more patriotic than the Eighth when it marched from Camp Alger. When they got to Cuba full of vigor there was no lagging and no straggling. As we marched from Siboney to Sevilla every man stuck to his work, hot as it was, because we were needed on the battle line. But the rains descended and in the floods was the disease that laid those young men low. Yet I never heard of homesickness once, until the poor, weak body could no longer control the mind. With fever all around, every last man stuck to his post, bravely and tenderly helping each other. Such men are heroes. It is the cool, calm facing of an unseen foe that tests courage. We will never forget the cause for which they died. With America's great power comes great responsibility. For downtrodden and suffering humanity they died or suffered. We will remember the midnight burial and all, and for them, if the call should come again, we would respond again as freely as they did last April.

"Religioso" by N. P. Chambers was the band's next selection—"Onward Christian Soldiers."

Lieut. Col. Charles Dick of Akron was cheered as he came forward. We thank you for this tribute which you pay the memory of our departed comrades. Nothing we can do, nothing we can say, will add to their glory or the valor of their deeds, but these will be to all a test of patriotism most eloquent, could we but tell what was in their hearts. In the cause of humanity they gave up all a man can give. The good mother weeps for her boy, but war is suffering. No great cause moves forward without it. It is the sacrifice for a cause that consecrates it. For this struggle we are a greater, better, and more united people. The blood of these heroes has deepened the red stripes in our flag. Their sufferings have enriched its blue field. Their sacrifices have purified the white in our glorious banner. When the stars and stripes was hoisted at Santiago, July 17, it signaled to more of humanity than ever before, more of humanity than they had ever known. We feel that these sacrifices must have been acceptable to God, and while remembering them let us dedicate ourselves once more to their patriotic purpose and to the uplifting of mankind everywhere.

Maj. Charles C. Weybrecht, of Alliance, commander of 3rd Battalion: We are gathered to pay the last tribute to the boys who have gone before, but the sisters, the mothers, and wives have suffered as much as the soldiers. He asked to have his further speech made by the Reverend Dr. H. L. Wiles, of Mansfield, who said: Our soldier boys have a warm place in our hearts. In our sanctuaries, in our homes, Sabbath after Sabbath, night and morning, day after day, you were remembered in our prayers. My heart was uplifted when I heard the officers of the Eighth recognize God's hand in this cause, and urge us to go forward to possess these lands for the world, for God. Is not a noble cause deserving of a noble sacrifice? Eternity will justify it all for the great interests. We extend our kindest sympathy for your losses. May God add his richest blessing.

"The Old Church Organ," by N. P. Chambers, was played by the band.

Col. Hard told of the midnight burials near Santiago, and one day when five of our men lay dead for burial, there came a man of God to us just when needed, a friend, a brother. Thus introduced, the regimental chaplain, the Reverend J. O. Campbell, D.D., United Presbyterian pastor in Wooster, said: I see a picture that suggests the strength and power of this nation, in these soldiers flanked by the home friends. We are girt about by the unseen presence of "just men made perfect." Give them a chance to tell us the great lessons for which they died. The greatest monuments are not stone, or metal, but in hearts and deeds. Egypt's monuments are buried in sand, but the men of the New Testament put their lives into deeds and will live forever. So these seventy-two men would wish to be remembered for the cause and purpose for which they perished. The people are the greatest thing in all nations. The true index of national greatness is the kind of men it grows. The American soldier is the best, because he has the manhood, the home behind him. We ought to be better men and women in this presence, or stand silent by those thirteen graves on Sevilla Hill. God should reap a mighty harvest from these seventy-two lives. My worthy predecessor, a man of God, teaches righteousness though gone. The Eighth Ohio's heroes have consecrated Cuba, the sea, and America, that righteousness and truth shall be shared by all the islands that shall come to us; not for commerce, but that men may come up higher, and that wherever is spoken a noble thought, men may be lifted up to better things.

"God be with You till We Meet Again" was the appropriate tribute by the band, followed by a touching prayer and benediction by the Reverend T. S. Struggles, Methodist pastor at Smithville. Then the band played "America," and the regimental bugle corps sounded the "Taps," the soldiers' mournful farewell to their dead, and the memorable service was a memory.

Appendix 2

Roster Eighth Ohio Volunteers

The following roster is based on *The Official Roster of Ohio Soldiers in the War with Spain: 1898–1899* (Columbus, Ohio General Assembly, 1916). But it differs in two particulars. The roster printed in 1916 was confusingly organized—by companies, and ranks and grades within companies, with privates listed in two groups according to whether they were recruits or belonged to the company at the beginning of the war, and with appendices for men who transferred, deserted, were discharged, or died. The roster that follows is a straight alphabetical listing. Moreover, the 1916 roster misspelled many names, and I have checked all names against regimental records in the National Archives (five volumes in Record Group 94). Even then there were problems, for company clerks in 1898 were not very trustworthy. None possessed a typewriter; it was only the beginning of the typewriter era so everything was handwritten. Some clerks wrote names casually, perhaps according to sound. In the hand of the time a "u" looked like an "n" and vice versa, and both could become an "a." I tried to verify names by checking signatures, but some men could barely write (and one could not, and made his "x"), in many instances men for some reason did not sign their names, and one company's records contained no signatures.

	Name	Home	Rank	Company
	Abrams, Ed T.	Ashland	pvt	C
*	Adams, William K.	Shreve	pvt	H
	Aderholt, Robert K.	Canton	pvt	I
	Airhart, Charles E.	Shreve	qm sgt	H
	Airhart, Harley H.	Shreve	cpl	H
	Alban, Harold G.	Perrysville	pvt	H
	Albright, Howard R.	Wooster	pvt	D
	Albright, Percy D.	East Liverpool	pvt	E
	Aldrich, Bert	Cleveland	pvt	K
	Alexander, Herbert C.	Medina	pvt	G
	Allison, George D.	Akron	pvt	B
	Allison, William	Canton	pvt	L
	Allmeroth, Ellsworth E.	Millersburg	pvt	H
	Altaffer, Rufus	Bucyrus	pvt	A
	Alvord, Joseph G.	Mansfield	qm sgt	M
	Anderson, Baird N.	East Liverpool	pvt	E
	Anderson, Bert A.	Big Prairie	pvt	H
	Anderson, George O.	East Liverpool	1st lt	E
	Anglemyer, Thurman L.	Alliance	pvt	K
	Anthony, Louis H.	Canton	pvt	F
	Arick, Bert F.	Orrville	pvt	G
*	Armstrong, Robert L.	Millersburg	pvt	H
	Armstrong, Thomas	Hayesville	pvt	C
	Atkins, Frank A.	Canton	pvt	F
	Atwell, Zaddock F.	Canton	pvt	L, hq
	Auginbaugh, William	Canton	pvt	L
	Auhl, Fred	Polk	pvt	C
	Austin, Rufus	Big Prairie	pvt	H
	Babcock, Charles J.	Canton	pvt	I
	Bachmann, Charles A.	Akron	pvt	B
	Bacon, Fred W.	Bucyrus	cpl	A
	Bahler, Charles	Canton	qm sgt	L
	Bailey, Rezin M.	Canton	qm sgt	hq
	Baird, Henry L.	Canton	pvt	F
	Baker, Fred	Alliance	cpl	K
	Balizet, August F.	Canton	pvt	L
	Balizet, John E.	Canton	pvt	L
	Ballard, Whitcomb A.	Alliance	cpl	K

* died

NAME	HOME	RANK	COMPANY
Bankerd, William W.	Alliance	pvt	K
Barber, Edward P.	Akron	pvt	B, hq
Bardo, Oby	Alliance	pvt	K
Barker, John D.	Canton	pvt	I
Barker, Oliver P.	East Liverpool	artificer	E
Barnard, Richard	Canton	pvt	L
Barnard, William E.	Wooster	1st lt	D
Barnes, John R.	Wooster	pvt	D
Barnhart, Charles W.	Wooster	pvt	D
Barrett, Perry	Perrysville	pvt	H
Barrick, Jacob	Polk	artificer	C
Barry, William E.	Shreve	pvt	H
Bartley, Charles E.	Alliance	pvt	K
Bauch, Joseph	Akron	pvt	G
Bauer, Ulrich	Bucyrus	pvt	A
Baughman, Almon J.	Wadsworth	cpl	G
Baughman, William H.	Wooster	pvt	D
Baylor, Lorenzo	Albion	cpl	C
Beam, William H.	Mansfield	pvt	M
Beaty, Thomas J.	East Liverpool	cpl	E
Beaumont, Clifford	Canton	pvt	L
Becker, Arthur	Bucyrus	pvt	A
Beckley, Willard K.	Wooster	pvt	D
Bedford, Frank	Shreve	pvt	H
Beelman, Charles C.	Mansfield	cpl	M
Beelman, Harry T.	Bucyrus	pvt	A
Beeman, Earl T.	Loudonville	pvt	H
Beer, Frederick T.	Bucyrus	cpl	A
Beer, William C.	Bucyrus	wagoner	A
Bell, Sherman W.	Ashland	pvt	C
Bell, Tom M.	Mansfield	cpl	M
Belzner, Charles F.	Bucyrus	pvt	A
Bender, Elwood C.	Akron	pvt	B
Berlin, Henry L.	Canton	pvt	L, deserted
Bernhard, Hugo A.	Canton	pvt	I
Berry, Ernest A.	Elyria	wagoner	H
Berry, Joseph B.	West Salem	pvt	C
Berry, Thomas	Bucyrus	pvt	A
Bertsch, Paul	Akron	pvt	B
Bessi, Joe	Canton	pvt	F
Betz, George H.	Canton	pvt	L
Beuchat, Henry	Canton	pvt	F

Name	Home	Rank	Company
Beverstock, Frank	Mansfield	cpl	M
Biddinger, Elmer R.	Sullivan	pvt	C
Biery, Philip	Canton	cpl	F
Bird, Charles E.	Loudonville	pvt	H
Birk, John W.	Bucyrus	1st lt	A
Bitter, Julius F.	Akron	pvt	B
Bittikofer, Charles L.	Bucyrus	pvt	A
Black, John P.	Canton	pvt	L
Blackburn, Harry J.	Akron	1st lt	B
Blake, George H.	Wooster	pvt	D
Blake, George T.	East Liverpool	sgt	E
* Bland, Ebbie N.	Bucyrus	pvt	A
Blinn, Albert H.	Canton	pvt	L
Bloodhart, Arthur C.	Bucyrus	pvt	A
Bloom, Geoffrey J.	Mansfield	pvt	M
Bloomfield, Clement O.	Canton	1st sgt	F
Bock, Charles G.	Canton	pvt	I
Bock, Otto	Canton	pvt	F
* Boden, Charles E.	Wadsworth	cpl	G
Bolender, Walter J.	Canton	pvt	F
Boles, Rice E.	Akron	pvt	B
Bolich, Herbert E.	Wadsworth	sgt, 1st lt	G
Bolich, William	Wadsworth	sgt	G
Bordner, Homer E.	Canton	pvt	L
Bordner, William H.	Akron	pvt	B
Bott, La Roy	Ashland	pvt	C
Bourguard, Edward E.	Columbus	pvt	K
Bowen, William	Canton	pvt	F
Bowman, Albert T.	Canton	pvt	I
Bowman, Curtis J.	Canton	cpl	K
Bowman, Robert H.	Akron	pvt	B
Boyd, William H.	Wooster	pvt	D
Boyle, John O.	Polk	pvt	C
Bradford, Walter S., Jr.	Mansfield	2d lt	M
Branstetter, Harry P.	Wooster	pvt	D
Breckenridge, William	Canton	cpl	F
Bressler, Roscoe L.	Canton	pvt	L
Breymaier, William J.	Bucyrus	pvt	A
Bricker, Altie L.	Akron	pvt	H
Bride, Harry M.	Mansfield	pvt	M

* died

NAME	HOME	RANK	COMPANY
Bride, Theodore	Mansfield	sgt	M, hq
Brink, Harold S.	Killbuck	cpl	H
Broeske, Henry	Canton	pvt	F
Brosius, Edgar E.	Alliance	1st lt	K
Brosius, Harry E.	Alliance	1st sgt	K
Brothers, Arthur M.	Canton	pvt	I
Brought, Frank H.	Medina	pvt	G
Brown, Daniel W.	Akron	batt sgt maj	hq
Brown, Fay W.	Bucyrus	pvt	A
Brown, Frank W.	Perrysville	pvt	H
Brown, George W.	Wooster	pvt	D
Brown, Gerald H.	Akron	pvt	B
Brown, Harry B.	Millersburg	pvt	H
Brown, John B.	Bucyrus	pvt	A
Brown, Nathan W.	Canton	pvt	I
Brown, Thomas B.	Shreve	pvt	H
Brown, Thomas D.	Wooster	pvt	D
Brown, Thomas P.	Wooster	pvt	D
Browning, John H.	Canton	pvt	L
Brownson, Charles W.	Lattasburg	pvt	C
* Bruce, Vincent E.	Mansfield	pvt	M
Brumbaugh, David J.	Akron	pvt	B
Brumbaugh, George F.	Seville	pvt	G
Bryan, Frederick C.	Akron	maj	hq
Bryan, John L.	New Baltimore	pvt	K
Bryan, Joseph C.	Polk	sgt	C
Bryant, Charles F.	Bucyrus	pvt	A
Buch, Victor F.	Canton	qm sgt	F
Buchanan, Frederick H.	Shreve	pvt	H
Bucher, William H., Jr.	Wooster	pvt	D
Buchman, John	Canton	pvt	I
Buchter, Stanley D.	Ashland	pvt	C
Buckholtz, Jacob	Akron	pvt	G
Buckwalter, Samuel W.	Canton	cook	I
Buel, Henry V.	Alliance	pvt	K, hosp
Burg, George	Wooster	pvt	D
Burgess, John	Akron	pvt	G
Burk, John	Barberton	pvt	G
Burklew, Sewell R.	Killbuck	musician	H, hq
Burla, Frank T.	Akron	pvt	B

* died

	NAME	HOME	RANK	COMPANY
	Burnett, William H.	Shreve	cpl	H
	Burroughs, Edgar A.	Bucyrus	artificer	A
	Burrows, Arthur	East Liverpool	pvt	E
	Burson, William M.	Canton	1st lt	L
	Burton, Ralph H.	Washington, D.C.	pvt	K
	Burwell, James B.	Canton	pvt	I
	Burwell, William M.	Bucyrus	lance cpl	A
*	Byrd, Fred B.	Mansfield	pvt	M
	Callaghan, Peter	Bucyrus	pvt	A
	Cameron, Nathaniel C.	Wooster	pvt	D
	Cameron, Robert J.	Wooster	cpl	D
	Cameron, Wilford E.	Akron	pvt	B
	Campbell, George W.	East Liverpool	pvt	E
	Campbell, Harry E.	Akron	pvt	B
	Campbell, James O.	Wooster	chaplain	hq
*	Campbell, Lowell E.	Canal Dover	pvt	G
	Campbell, Robert J.	Shreve	sgt	H
	Campbell, Walter	Shreve	sgt	H
	Campbell, Walter G.	Washington, D.C.	pvt	K
	Cannon, Benjamin	Alliance	pvt	K
	Cantleberry, Joseph N.	Canton	pvt	F
	Carle, Chris	Bucyrus	pvt	A
*	Carnahan, David B.	East Liverpool	pvt	K
	Carnahan, Morris J.	East Liverpool	pvt	E
*	Carpenter, John L.	Loudonville	pvt	C
	Carpenter, Joseph W.	Killbuck	pvt	H
	Carr, Don M.	Canton	cpl	I
	Carr, Sherman H.	Wooster	pvt	D
	Carrick, Thomas A.	Mansfield	pvt	M
	Carson, John S.	Canton	pvt	I
	Cass, Claude A.	Akron	cpl	B
	Caton, Harry A.	East Liverpool	pvt	E
	Chaddock, Ollie	Canton	pvt	F
	Chambers, Will M.	Canton	pvt	L
	Chandler, Percy A.	East Liverpool	pvt	L
	Chapin, Robert H.	Akron	pvt	B
	Charlton, Marquis A.	Bucyrus	capt	A
	Charlton, Wilber J.	Bucyrus	pvt	A

* died

	Name	Home	Rank	Company
	Chatlain, Charles E.	Mansfield	pvt	M
	Cheveraux, Paul S.	Canton	musician	I, hq
	Christensen, Charles F.	Akron	pvt	B
	Christie, Robert L.	Bucyrus	pvt	A
	Christine, Louis W.	Wooster	pvt	D
	Christopher, Albert	Millersburg	pvt	H
	Christopher, Calvin	Millersburg	pvt	H
	Christopher, Charles C.	Millersburg	pvt	H
	Christy, Charles W.	Wooster	pvt	D
	Chubb, Frederick A.	Oakland, Calif.	pvt	C
	Clapsaddle, John H.	Alliance	cpl	K
	Clark, Jerome E.	Wooster	pvt	D
	Clark, Jess M.	Ashland	qm sgt	C
	Clark, Joseph	Akron	pvt	B
	Clark, Scott A.	Sullivan	pvt	C
	Clark, William A.	Canton	cpl	L
	Clark, William W., Jr.	Canton	pvt	I
	Clarke, Claude B.	Akron	pvt	B
*	Clay, Alvin B.	Wooster	pvt	D
	Clay, Uriah E.	Canton	cpl	L
	Clewell, Charles E.	Shreve	pvt	H
	Clewell, Charles W.	Canton	sgt	F
	Cline, Jerry	Akron	pvt	B
	Close, William M.	Millersburg	pvt	H
	Closson, John D.	Ashland	pvt	C
	Clugston, James V.	Ashland	pvt	C
	Coffee, Richard W.	Alliance	pvt	K
	Cole, Elmer L.	Killbuck	pvt	H
	Cole, James R.	Shreve	cpl	H
	Cole, William A.	Akron	pvt	B
	Coleman, George O.	Bucyrus	pvt	A
*	Coleman, George W.	Mansfield	pvt	M
	Coleman, John W.	Canton	cpl	F
	Colesworthy, William C.	Mansfield	pvt	M
	Connelly, Freeman E.	Columbus	pvt	M
	Conrad, Edward D.	Wooster	pvt	D
	Conrad, Harry E.	Canton	pvt	L
	Conrad, Kirk H.	Lansing, Mich.	pvt	G
	Conrad, Willie A.	Wooster	artificer	D
	Converse, Norris M.	Canton	sgt	I
	Cook, Van C.	Mansfield	pvt	M

* died

NAME	HOME	RANK	COMPANY
Cook, Walter S.	East Liverpool	cpl	E
Cooper, Charles F.	Alliance	qm sgt	K
Cooper, Heber	Akron	musician	C, hq
Copthorne, Harold S.	Canton	cpl	I
Corey, James A.	Canton	pvt	I
Corey, William E.	Canton	pvt	I
Coulter, Edward J.	Bucyrus	pvt	A
Couts, Harry	Bucyrus	pvt	A
Cowley, George A.	Canton	pvt	L
Cox, Charles C.	East Liverpool	pvt	E
Cox, William G.	East Liverpool	pvt	E
Coyle, John W.	Akron	musician	G, hq
Craig, Frank	Mansfield	pvt	M
Cramer, John C.	Bucyrus	sgt	A
Cranz, Clarence	Akron	sgt	B
Cranz, Earl	Akron	qm sgt	B
Creath, Owen W.	Wooster	pvt	D
Creighton, Ossian C.	Akron	pvt	B
Crewson, Walter S.	Steubenville	pvt	E
Criley, Wallace K.	Wooster	pvt	D
Crim, John B.	Bucyrus	cpl	A
Critchfield, Ammon B.	Shreve	capt	H
Critchfield, Benjamin H.	Loudonville	pvt	H
Critchfield, Lyman R., Jr.	Wooster	pvt	D
Croker, John W.	Plimpton (Plymouth?)	pvt	H
Crowl, Calvin D.	Alliance	artificer	K
Crowl, Isaac W.	Alliance	pvt	K
* Crubaugh, Clyde B.	Alliance	sgt	K
Crum, Thomas M.	Canton	wagoner	I
Crumrine, Charles C.	Akron	cpl	B
Culberson, Elmer L.	Alliance	pvt	K
Culp, John C.	Mansfield	pvt	M
Culp, William A.	Mansfield	artificer	M
Cumberland, Charles E.	Wooster	pvt	D
Cumberland, LaVern C.	Wooster	cpl	D
Cummins, William M.	Bucyrus	pvt	A
Cunin, Austin E.	Canton	pvt	F
Cunningham, Oliver M.	Wadsworth	pvt	G
Curley, Harry O.	Canton	pvt	L
Curran, John	Mansfield	pvt	M
Curry, Will R.	Wooster	cpl	D

* died

NAME	HOME	RANK	COMPANY
Dagenhard, Henry	Wadsworth	pvt	G
Daniels, John W.	Canton	pvt	L
Dannemiller, Augustus F., Jr.	Canton	pvt	I
Darling, William M.	Perrysville	pvt	H
Dauber, John G.	Canton	pvt	I
Daugherty, Harry F.	Mansfield	pvt	M
Davis, Harry K.	East Liverpool	pvt	E
Davis, Herbert C.	Alliance	pvt	K
Davis, James F.	Canton	cpl	F
Davis, Joseph C.	East Liverpool	cpl	E
Davis, Louis J.	Alliance	pvt	K
Day, Charles	Mansfield	pvt	M
Deam, William C.	Bucyrus	pvt	A
Deardorff, Charles W.	Bucyrus	musician	A
Deckman, Arthur W.	Canton	pvt	F
Deibler, Tully O.	Polk	capt	C
Delaney, Thomas E.	Canton	pvt	F
Delp, Henry	Canton	pvt	L
DeMuth, Benjamin A.	Canton	sgt	I
Depler, Frank	Rowsburg	pvt	C
Derr, Eddie W.	Wooster	pvt	D
Derry, Lawrence	Big Prairie	pvt	H
Dever, Bernard E.	Alliance	pvt	K
Dewar, James H.	East Liverpool	pvt	E, hq
Dibble, Fred C.	Wadsworth	cpl	G
Dibble, Harry H.	Wadsworth	cpl	G
Dice, Arch H.	Wooster	1st sgt	D
Dick, Charles W.F.	Akron	lt col	hq
Dick, Frank P.	Wadsworth	pvt	G
Dick, James E.	Wadsworth	cpl	G
Dickson, Robert T.	Akron	cpl	B
Didion, William	Akron	artificer	B
Diehl, Fred H.	Akron	pvt	B
Dieringer, Edward H.	Canton	pvt	I
Dinkel, Christopher	Bucyrus	cpl	A
Diveler, Amos M.	Polk	pvt	C
Dix, Martin W.	Millersburg	pvt	H
Dobson, David D.	Alliance	pvt	K
Dobson, Harry M.	Alliance	sgt	K
Dodd, Carroll L.	East Liverpool	pvt	E
Doll, Kent	Canton	pvt	L
Donald, Harry C.	Millersburg	pvt	H
Donnenwirth, Clarence F.	Bucyrus	pvt	A

NAME	HOME	RANK	COMPANY
Donze, Albert	Canton	pvt	F
Donze, Julius E.	Canton	pvt	I
Dorman, William C.	Mansfield	pvt	M
Dorrance, John M.	Akron	pvt	B
Douglas, Neal	Alliance	cpl	K
Douglass, Harvey C.	Millersburg	pvt	H
Douglass, William H.	Millersburg	pvt	H
Downs, Robert F.	Ashland	pvt	C
Draime, Frank J.	Canton	pvt	L
Dreenen, Martin W.	Canton	pvt	I, hosp
Driscoll, Robert	East Liverpool	pvt	E
Drushal, David H.	Wooster	musician	D, hq
Duer, Joseph D.	Millersburg	cpl	H
Duke, Charles W.	East Liverpool	pvt	E
Dulabahn, Henry K.	Canton	pvt	L
Dunn, James	Sharon (Center ?)	pvt	G
Durant, George L.	Akron	pvt	B
Dye, Frank S.	East Liverpool	pvt	E
Dyer, Ward B.	Canton	pvt	I
Eaby, Harry P.	Wooster	sgt	D
Eakins, Burt H.	Akron	pvt	B, hosp
Eberhart, Galilean C.	Shreve	artificer	H
Eberly, George	Loudonville	pvt	H
Ebner, Clement J.	Wadsworth	pvt	G
* Eck, Michael	East Liverpool	pvt	E
Eckert, Calvin	Alliance	pvt	K
Eckis, Ezra L.	Mansfield	pvt	M
* Eckley, Frank	Canton	pvt	F
Eckstine, Frank	Canton	pvt	F
* Eddy, Okey J.	East Liverpool	pvt	E
Eddy, Ralph W.	Wooster	pvt	D
Edleman, Charles N.	Canton	pvt	I
Edwards, Orla P.	Albion	cpl	C
Edwards Orland R.	Polk	2d lt	C
Eells, Milton R.	Alliance	pvt	K
Egner, Otis J.	Olivesburg	pvt	C
Eidt, John M.	Polk	sgt	C
Emerick, Edward E.	Wooster	pvt	D
Emerson, Guy P.	Bucyrus	pvt	A

* died

	Name	Home	Rank	Company
	Enhart, Harry	Akron	pvt	B
	Eoff, Harry	East Liverpool	pvt	E
	Eoff, William M.	East Liverpool	pvt	E
	Erdman, Walter L.	Canton	pvt	I
	Eschliman, David	Canton	sgt	F
	Essner, Joseph G.	Canton	pvt	I
	Ewing, Thomas C.	Ashland	pvt	C
	Fahr, Ilger C.	Redhaw	cpl	C
	Fair, Thomas	East Liverpool	pvt	E
	Falor, Clarence E.	Akron	pvt	G
	Farmer, Harry	East Liverpool	pvt	E
*	Farquhar, Emmer C.	Zanesville	maj and surg	hq
	Farrell, Frank	Canton	pvt	F
	Farver, Cyrus W.	Millersburg	pvt	H
	Faubel, Charles W.	Canton	pvt	L
	Feederle, Herman O.	Akron	capt	B
	Ferguson, Clark E.	Canton	sgt	F
	Ferguson, Sherman	Medina	pvt	G
	Ferrall, Charles	Columbus	pvt	A
	Fidler, Charles	Bucyrus	pvt	A
	Filliez, George E.	Canton	pvt	F
	Fiscus, Stanton C.	Wadsworth	pvt	G
	Fisher, Cyrus H.	Bucyrus	pvt	A
	Fisher, Elmer D.	Mansfield	pvt	M
	Fisher, Marcus A.	Canton	capt	L
	Fitler, Jacob P.	Wooster	pvt	D
	Flanagan, Barney	Canton	pvt	F
	Flinn, James G.	Ashland	pvt	C
	Flory, Charles W.	Canton	pvt	L
	Foreman, Charles W.	Bucyrus	pvt	A
	Foreman, Homer A.	Bucyrus	pvt	A
	Fortney, Charles L.	Wooster	pvt	D
	Fouche, Ira	Wadsworth	pvt	G
	Frankeberger, William	Mansfield	cpl	M
*	Frazier, Charles W.	Wooster	pvt	D
	Freed, Preston C.	Canton	pvt	I
	Freeman, Thomas G.	Canton	pvt	F
	Fretter, Albert H.	Medina	pvt	G

* died

Name	Home	Rank	Company
Frick, Frank F.	Dayton	pvt	G
Fry, Alvin, C.	Ashland	pvt	C
Fulton, James E.	Bucyrus	principal musician	hq
Funk, Earl P.	Medina	cpl	G
Funk, Sterling R.	Wooster	cpl	D
Gailey, John B.	Mansfield	sgt	M
* Gallagher, Nicholas	Wadsworth	pvt	G
Galloway, Robert A.	Akron	pvt	B
* Gardner, Alfred G.	Ashland	pvt	C
Garman, Charles W.	Akron	pvt	B
Gasche, Louis E.	Wooster	sgt	D
Gates, Charles A.	Mansfield	pvt	M
Gaudert, John W.	Mansfield	cpl	M
Geary, Herb	Hayesville	pvt	C
Genet, Edward	Millersburg	pvt	H
Geoghan, Edward	Canton	pvt	L
George, John	Canton	pvt	L
Gerhart, Woodbury W.	West Salem	pvt	C
Gerlach, Frank C.	Wooster	capt	D
Gersinger, Frank F.	Akron	pvt	G
Gerstenschlager, Valentine, Jr.	Wadsworth	cpl	G
Gerstner, Edward H.	Akron	pvt	G
Getz, John W.	Loudonville	pvt	H
Geukes, William D.	Canton	pvt	L
* Gibler, Frank	Canton	pvt	I
Gibson, Louis R.	Sullivan	pvt	C
Gibson, Ralph S.	Canton	pvt	I
Gilbert, Robert S.	Alliance	pvt	K
Gilhuly, Joseph A.	Alliance	pvt	K
Gilletly, Fred	Ashland	pvt	C
Gilson, John R.	East Liverpool	wagoner	E
Gladfelter, Fred A.	Steubenville	pvt	E
Glenn, Charles E.	Alliance	pvt	K
Glenn, Joseph T.	Wooster	pvt	D
Glenn, Samuel M., Jr.	Wooster	pvt	D
Glessner, Eugene C.	Polk	sgt	C
Gloss, William H.	Canton	pvt	F
Goddard, Frank C.	Akron	pvt	B

* died

NAME	HOME	RANK	COMPANY
Good, Charles W.	Wadsworth	pvt	G
Goodyear, Ira	Canton	cpl	F
Gorham, John D.	Sullivan	pvt	C
Gotshall, Charles E.	Canton	sgt	L
Grable, Albert C.	Canton	pvt	I
Graham, Charles R.	Canton	cpl	L
Graham, Harry	Akron	pvt	G
Graham, William B.	Canton	sgt	L
Gravatt, Quintin M.	Wooster	pvt	D
Graves, William W.	Wooster	pvt	D
Gray, Frank G.	Wooster	pvt	D
Green, Heber S.	East Liverpool	pvt	F
Greenwald, Howard M.	Canton	cpl	L
Grether, Lewis J.	Akron	cpl	B
Griest, James E.	Wooster	pvt	D
Griffith, Harry E.	Alliance	pvt	K
Grimes, Lawrence H.	Alliance	pvt	K
Griner, Grant S.	Polk	cpl	C
Groesel, Ernest	Akron	pvt	B
Grossenbach, Cary W.	Wooster	cpl	D
Grossklaus, William	Canton	pvt	F
Groth, John	Canton	pvt	I
Grubb, Loyal	Alliance	cpl	K
Grunau, Bruno	Canton	pvt	F
Gunsaulis, William	Wadsworth	pvt	G
Gustafson, Ernst	Canton	pvt	F
Gween, Herman H.	Canton	pvt	F
Gyger, Elliott L.	Alliance	capt	K
Haase, Carl A.	Akron	pvt	I
Haase, Rudolph W.	Akron	pvt	I
Hackathorn, Joseph H.	East Liverpool	pvt	E
Hackett, Martin J.	Mansfield	pvt	M
Hackworth, William G.	East Liverpool	cpl	E
Haden, Harry	East Liverpool	pvt	E
Hadley, Glen W.	Canton	pvt	I
Hadley, William S.	Canton	pvt	I
Haffner, Luther	Bucyrus	pvt	A
* Hagaman, Frank J.	Canton	pvt	F

* died

	Name	Home	Rank	Company
	Hagan, Henry H.	Canton	pvt	L
*	Hague, Harry G.	Shreve	pvt	H
	Hagy, Homer C.	Canton	pvt	I
	Hagy, William E.	Canton	cpl	I
	Hale, Frank T.	East Liverpool	pvt	E
	Hall, Charles	Mansfield	cpl	M
	Hall, Robert T.	East Liverpool	2d lt	E
	Hambleton, Thomas	Wadsworth	sgt	G
	Hambley, Charles H.	Akron	pvt	G
	Hanley, William F.	East Liverpool	1st sgt	E
	Hanna, Robert H.	Millersburg	pvt	H
	Hans, John R.	Canton	sgt	L
	Hanscom, Austin B.	Akron	pvt	B
*	Happer, George L.	Millersburg	pvt	H
	Harbaugh, Wade	Mansfield	pvt	M
*	Harbet, Charles	Canton	pvt	F
	Hard, Curtis V.	Wooster	col	hq
	Hard, Dudley J.	Wooster	1st lt	I
	Hardgrove, Burton C.	Canton	pvt	I
	Harding, Charles S.	Canton	pvt	L
	Harding, Elmer F.	Canton	pvt	I
	Harding, Howard A.	Canton	pvt	I
	Harding, William H.	Akron	pvt	B
	Harmon, Russell P.	Rowsburg	pvt	C
	Harpster, Bert F.	Jeromesville	pvt	C
	Harrington, Alfred	Mansfield	cpl	M
	Harrington, Ralph E.	Canton	pvt	I, hosp
	Harris, Walter H.	Akron	musician	H, hq
	Harter, Rollin E.	Wadsworth	pvt	G
	Hartman, William V.	Mansfield	pvt	M
	Hartsel, Frank L.	Polk	sgt	C
	Harvey, Bert	Canton	pvt	F
	Harvey, Joseph B.	East Liverpool	pvt	E
	Hastings, Thomas F.	Mansfield	pvt	M
	Hauptfner, Edward	Canton	pvt	F
*	Haushalter, Fred	Akron	pvt	B
	Hayes, Frederick, Jr.	Ashland	pvt	C
	Hayman, Roy H.	Bucyrus	pvt	A
	Haynes, George J.	Mansfield	pvt	M
*	Heacock, James B.	Alliance	pvt	K

* died

NAME	HOME	RANK	COMPANY
Headley, Harry E.	East Liverpool	pvt	E
Headley, John C.	East Liverpool	pvt	E
Heater, Charles A.	Wooster	musician	D
Heaton, Hugh	Alliance	pvt	K
Hedd, William P.	Wadsworth	pvt	G
Heddleson, Lawrence E.	East Liverpool	cpl	E
Heddleston, Edgar H.	East Liverpool	pvt	E
Heer, George	Alliance	2d lt	K
Heidinger, Andrew	Mansfield	pvt	M
Heifner, Elza	Jeromesville	pvt	C
Heintz, Albert	Bucyrus	pvt	A
Heisler, Jacob W.	Canton	pvt	I
Helbling, Charles T.	Akron	pvt	B
* Heller, Alex	Akron	pvt	B
Heller, Harry M.	Wooster	pvt	D
Hemperly, Clarence E.	Canton	pvt	F
Henning, Harry F.	Canton	pvt	F
Henry, Charles E.	East Liverpool	pvt	E
Hensel, Rolland V.	Shreve	pvt	H
Hentzell, Benjamin F.	Canton	pvt	L
Herdlicka, Jared	Canton	cpl	L
Herdlicka, Joseph	Canton	cpl	L
Herrington, Bert B.	Wadsworth	pvt	G
Hershey, Benjamin F.	Canton	pvt	I
Herst, Charles E.	Creston	pvt	G
Hess, James	Polk	1st sgt	C
Hetzel, John	Akron	pvt	B
Hetzel, Peter	Ashland	cpl	C
Hewitt, James H.	Canton	pvt	F
Hider, Clarence A.	West Salem	pvt	C
Hieronimus, Joseph J.	Bucyrus	pvt	A
Hile, Fred C.	Wadsworth	1st lt	G
Hill, Frank H.	Bucyrus	cpl	A
Hill, James P.	Bucyrus	pvt	A
Hill, John M.	Canton	musician	F
Hill, William M.	East Liverpool	capt	E
Hillis, Emmer G.	Bucyrus	pvt	A
Hillis, William D.	Bucyrus	pvt	A
Hiltabidle, Guy P.	Mansfield	pvt	M
Hinkle, Oliver C.	Canton	pvt	F

* died

NAME	HOME	RANK	COMPANY
Hine, Peter V.	Mansfield	sgt	M
Hipp, Michael	Bucyrus	pvt	A
Hissner, Elmer A.	Alliance	pvt	K
Hites, Emanuel	Holmesville	pvt	H
Hoagland, Harry D.	Akron	cpl	B
Hobbs, Wilbert A.	East Liverpool	surg	hq
Hockensmith, Charles A.	Ashland	pvt	C
Hoff, Rollo D.	East Liverpool	pvt	E
Hogan, Patrick A.	Mansfield	pvt	M
Holland, Harry H.	Bucyrus	pvt	A
Holloway, Albert C.	Akron	pvt	B
* Holloway, Edwin C.	Wellsville	pvt	E
Holman, John W.	Canton	sgt	L
Holsington, Fin H.	Wadsworth	pvt	G
Honodle, Edward	Akron	pvt	B
Hoover, Charles S.	Alliance	sgt maj, 2d lt	G, hq
Hoover, Harold	Shreve	pvt	H
Hoppes, Lucius	Alliance	pvt	K
Hopusch, Fred	Canton	pvt	I
Horn, Franklin B.	Wooster	sgt	D
Horn, Webster D.	Wooster	cpl	D
* Hoshour, David F.	Canton	pvt	I
Hoslar, John H.	Canton	pvt	F
Hosler, Elza	Jeromesville	pvt	C
Hostetter, Frank I.	Canton	pvt	L
Hougland, Harley	Akron	pvt	B
Houser, Charles J.	Canton	sgt	I
Howard, John A.	East Liverpool	pvt	E
* Hoyer, Harry B.	Mansfield	cpl	M
Hoyt, Joel W.	East Liverpool	pvt	E
Hubbell, Walter M.	Bucyrus	pvt	A
Huber, Jacob	Bucyrus	pvt	A
Hudnut, Charles W.	Holmesville	pvt	H
Hudson, James A.	Canton	1st sgt	L
Huffman, Charles S.	Medina	pvt	G
Huffman, Edward E.	Wadsworth	pvt	G
Huggins, John B.	Mansfield	1st sgt	M
Hughes, Charles H.	Mansfield	1st lt	M
Hughes, John H.	East Liverpool	pvt	E

* died

Name	Home	Rank	Company
Hughes, William H.	Wooster	pvt	D
Hull, Hugh B.	Mansfield	pvt	M
Humiston, Alva S.	Bucyrus	sgt	A
Hunsberger, Walter W.	Wadsworth	1st sgt	G
Hunt, Ernest L.	Wadsworth	pvt	G
Hurford, William P.	Canton	cpl	F
Huston, Charles H.	Mansfield	cpl	M
Hutson, George K.	Alliance	cpl	K
Hutson, Jesse P.	Alliance	pvt	K
* Immler, O. Earl	Wooster	pvt	D
Irvin, Charles F.	Mansfield	pvt	M
Ish, Bert	Akron	pvt	G
Jackson, William W.	East Liverpool	pvt	E
Jacobs, Harry A.	Wooster	pvt	D
Jahant, George A.	Canton	pvt	L
Jarrett, William S.	Alliance	sgt	K
Jarvis, Arthur	Shreve	pvt	H
Jarvis, Clarence J.	Hayesville	pvt	C
Jeppson, Charles J.	Akron	pvt	B
Johnson, Arthur C.	Akron	pvt	B
Johnson, Merten R.	Wooster	pvt	D
Johnson, William C.	Mansfield	pvt	M
Johnston, Charles R.	Mansfield	pvt	M
Jolliff, Harvey F.	Wooster	pvt	D
Jones, Albert H.	Huntington	wagoner	C
Jones, Alfred M.	Akron	pvt	B
Jones, Benjamin D.	Canton	pvt	F, hosp
Jones, Charles V.	Columbus	pvt	A
Jones, Edward W.	Alliance	pvt	K
Jones, Samuel T.	Millersburg	pvt	H
Jones, Thomas	East Liverpool	pvt	E
Jones, William	Akron	pvt	B
Joseph, William	Akron	pvt	B
Kahler, Samuel	Bucyrus	pvt	A
* Kaiser, Asa B.	Springville	pvt	H

* died

	NAME	HOME	RANK	COMPANY
	Kaiser, Harmon	Canton	pvt	L
	Kanary, Pat	Mansfield	pvt	M
	Karg, William	Mansfield	pvt	M
	Karn, Harvey	Canton	pvt	I
	Karn, James D.	Canton	pvt	I
*	Kaufman, Arthur L.	Mansfield	pvt	M
	Keck, Harry E.	Akron	pvt	B
	Keefer, Joseph W.	Wadsworth	pvt	G
	Kehner, George	Bucyrus	pvt	A
	Keiser, Rudolph	Canton	pvt	L
	Keister, Charles W.	Shreve	pvt	H
	Kelley, Charles E.	Alliance	pvt	K
	Kempel, Joseph, Jr.	Akron	pvt	B
	Kerr, E. Harry	Bucyrus	pvt	A
	Kerr, Harry G.	East Liverpool	cpl	E
	Kerr, Robert W.	Bucyrus	cpl	A
	Kershew, Edward	Alliance	pvt	K
	Kessler, George	Mansfield	pvt	M
	Kidd, Samuel M.	Holmesville	pvt	H
*	Kieffer, Isaiah N.	Wooster	chaplain	hq
	King, Charles E.	Akron	pvt	B
	King, Jesse W.	Akron	cpl	B
	King, Rufus H.	Mansfield	cpl	M
	Kingsworth, Harvey Z.	Canton	pvt	L
	Kinkler, Harry	Wooster	pvt	D
	Kinninger, George E.	Bucyrus	cpl	A
	Kinsey, William H.	East Liverpool	sgt	E
*	Kiplinger, Charles C.	Bucyrus	pvt	A
	Kiplinger, Don T.	Polk	cpl	C
	Kirkwood, Allie M.	Wellsville	pvt	E
	Kirkwood, Daniel E.	Alliance	pvt	K
	Kister, Melville S.	Millbrook	pvt	H
	Kistler, Joseph W.	Wooster	pvt	D
	Knapp, Alexander	Mansfield	pvt	M
	Knorzer, Ludwig	Canton	pvt	F
	Knoth, William F.	Ashland	pvt	C
*	Knowles, William R.	Alliance	cpl	K
	Koehler, Percy B.	Canton	pvt	I
	Koenig, Max V.	Canton	pvt	F
	Kolp, Willard E.	Ashland	pvt	C

* died

NAME	HOME	RANK	COMPANY
Koons, Glenn	Bucyrus	pvt	A
Koons, Harry J.	Columbus	musician	M
Koontz, William H.	Canton	pvt	I
Kopp, Clarence E.	Redhaw	cpl	C
* Kosht, Guy G.	Canton	pvt	I
Kostenbader, Frank	Wooster	pvt	D
Kostenbader, John W.	Wooster	pvt	H
Kramer, Ezra	Rowsburg	pvt	C
Kraska, August	Mansfield	pvt	M
Kraver, Charles W.	Akron	cpl	B
Kraver, Fred W.	Medina	pvt	G
Kreider, Fred W.	Wadsworth	pvt	G
Kreighbaum, Frank	Columbus	pvt	K
Kress, John C.	Canton	pvt	F
Kuhlman, Howard W.	Canton	pvt	I
Kuhn, Edward G.	Big Prairie	pvt	H
Kuhns, Herman L.	Canton	capt and qm	hq
Kutz, Frank	Canton	pvt	F
* LaLone, Peter C.	Ashland	pvt	C
Lamberton, James C.	Mansfield	pvt	M
Landers, John F.	Wooster	pvt	H
Langell, Clement E.	Wooster	pvt	D
Lape, John H., Jr.	Canton	pvt	L
Lape, Melvin B.	Canton	cpl	L
Lautenschlager, Harvey	Millersburg	pvt	H
Lautz, Charles W.	Akron	pvt	F, hq
* Lautzenheiser, Irwin	Wooster	pvt	D
Lautzenheiser, Perrine	Wooster	cpl	D
Lawrence, Birdsell S.	Mansfield	pvt	M
Leach, Coleman	Hayesville	pvt	C
Leahy, William P.	Canton	cpl	F
Leapold, Frederick J.	Wooster	pvt	D
Lee, Bennie	Canton	pvt	I
Lee, Ernest R.	Seville	pvt	G
Lee, Frank C.	Wadsworth	capt	G
* Lee, John S.	Easton	cpl	G
Leeper, William H.	Millbrook	pvt	H
Lefevre, Harry E.	Ashland	pvt	C

* died

	NAME	HOME	RANK	COMPANY
	LeGraen, Alfred H.	Alliance	pvt	K
	Lehman, Harry J.	Wooster	pvt	H
*	Leininger, John A.	Canton	capt	F
*	Leininger, William	Huntington	pvt	C
	Leitz, Harry W.	Bucyrus	pvt	A
	Lerch, William G.	Wooster	pvt	D
	Lerson, Arthur	Ashland	pvt	C
	Leslie, Darragh	Canton	pvt	L
	Leslie, Levi	Canton	pvt	L
	Leu, Harry W.	Alliance	cpl	K
	Lewis, Raymond E.	Akron	pvt	B
*	Lillich, Daniel	Akron	pvt	B
	Limb, George S.	Wooster	qm sgt	D
	Linberger, Charles W.	Wooster	pvt	D
	Lindsey, Elmer F.	Mansfield	pvt	M
	Linn, Nelson F.	Canton	pvt	I
	Linton, Harry W.	Akron	pvt	H
	Lippoldt, Charles H.	Canton	pvt	L
	Little, Robert	Canton	pvt	F
	Locke, August E.	Canton	pvt	F
	Logan, Otis E.	Alliance	pvt	K
	Loller, Harry D.	Holmesville	pvt	H
	Long, Col. LeRoy	Ashland	pvt	C
*	Long, John C.	Acme	cpl	G
	Long, Oscar W.	Sullivan	pvt	C
	Long, William A.	Wadsworth	pvt	G
	Longacre, Ellsworth H.	Akron	pvt	B
	Longley, George	Canton	pvt	L
	Loomis, Albert K.	Medina	artificer	G
	Lormer, Robert A.	Canton	pvt	I
	Lothamer, Philip J.	Canton	pvt	I
	Love, William H.	Akron	pvt	B
	Lowery, Dennis	Mansfield	pvt	M
	Lowry, Robert H.	Mansfield	pvt	M
	Lowther, Robert W.	Alliance	pvt	K
	Lucas, Isaiah	East Liverpool	pvt	E
	McCallum, William M.	Alliance	pvt	K
	McCarron, Dennis M.	East Liverpool	pvt	E

---

* died

	Name	Home	Rank	Company
	McClarran, Harry L.	Wooster	pvt	D
	McClelland, William G.	Wooster	pvt	D
	McCord, William R.	East Liverpool	cpl	E
	McCowan, Charles H.	Alliance	pvt	K
	McCoy, Charles A.	Canton	cpl	I
	McCracken, Jay C.	Bucyrus	pvt	A
	McCray, Benjamin W.	Ashland	pvt	C
	McCrory, Charles J.	Hayesville	pvt	C
*	McDowell, Moses	Shreve	pvt	H
	McFarland, Harry W.	Mansfield	pvt	M
	McGaffic, Wilmer	Canton	pvt	F
	McGill, Thomas G.	East Liverpool	pvt	E
	McGirr, James S.	Alliance	pvt	K
	McGowan, Frank A.	Camp Alger, Va.	pvt	I, hosp
*	McGrath, James L.	Canton	pvt	F
	McIntosh, John P.	East Liverpool	pvt	E
	McIntyre, Charles G.	Orrville	pvt	G
	McKay, William K.	Mansfield	pvt	M
	McKee, Frank S.	West Salem	pvt	C
	McKeehen, Gilbert	Bucyrus	pvt	A
	McKinley, James F.	Camp Alger, Va.	pvt	I
	McKinney, Charles H.	Wooster	pvt	D
	McKinney, Frederick S.	Wooster	hosp steward	hq
	McKinney, William H.	East Liverpool	pvt	E
	McKinnon, Cash	Canton	pvt	F
	McKinnon, John C.D.	East Liverpool	pvt	E
	McKinnon, Orville J.	East Liverpool	pvt	E
	Mackley, Joseph H.	Mansfield	pvt	M
	McLaughlin, Rodney	Canton	pvt	L
	McMahon, Peter	Mansfield	pvt	M
	McNamara, Herbert V.	Millersburg	cpl	H
	McPherren, James W.	Mansfield	pvt	M
	McQuillin, Willard	Hayesville	pvt	C
	McTammany, John	Akron	pvt	E, hq
	Maquire, Joseph	Mansfield	pvt	M
	Mahaney, Edward	Wooster	pvt	D
	Maiers, Harry	Canton	pvt	F
	Maize, Percy M.	Wooster	pvt	D
	Manley, William	Canton	pvt	F
	Manson, John C.	Shreve	cpl	H

* died

Name	Home	Rank	Company
Manson, Samuel N.	Shreve	sgt	H
Marchand, Aubrey W.	Canton	pvt	I, hosp
Markley, Joseph C.	Wadsworth	pvt	G
Marks, William M.	Overton	cpl	C
Marpe, Theodore	Canton	pvt	L
Marquis, Fred S.	Mansfield	capt	M
Martin, Frederick A.	East Liverpool	cook	E
Martin, John	Orrville	pvt	G
Massa, Albert H.	Mansfield	pvt	M
Mast, Emanuel T.	Millersburg	pvt	H
Maus, Walter B.	Alliance	pvt	K
Maxwell, Allen C.	Millersburg	pvt	H
Maxwell, Curtis, B.	Jeromesville	pvt	C
Maynes, Alexander W.	Akron	capt and adj	hq
Meeker, Carl S.	Canton	pvt	F
Meister, George	Canton	pvt	F
Merchant, Joseph U.	Canton	pvt	I
Merfeld, Joseph	Wadsworth	pvt	G
Merkel, Eugene D.	Shreve	sgt	H
Merillet, Oliver	Millersburg	pvt	H
Metz, Fred T.	Canton	pvt	L
Metzger, Augustus H.	Canton	pvt	F
Miday, Eugene J.	Canton	pvt	L
Milbourn, Edmund	Akron	pvt	B
Milham, Arthur R.	Wooster	pvt	D
Millar, Denton J.	Polk	pvt	C
Miller, Bert	East Liverpool	pvt	C
Miller, Bert	Shreve	pvt	H
* Miller, Charles F.	Ashland	pvt	C
Miller, Edward H.	Wooster	pvt	D
Miller, Eugene	Akron	pvt	G
Miller, Harry C.	Canton	pvt	I
Miller, Harry C.	Wooster	pvt	D
Miller, Henry N.	Shreve	cpl	H
Miller, Horace W.	Wooster	sgt	D
Miller, Maurice E.	Spencer	pvt	C
Miller, Orva	Alliance	pvt	K
Miller, Peter E.	Shreve	1st sgt	H
Miller, Ralph C.	Mansfield	pvt	M, hq
Miller, Roscoe C.	Canton	pvt	L

* died

NAME	HOME	RANK	COMPANY
Miller, Wallace	Alliance	cpl	K
Miller, William H.	Canton	artificer	F
Miller, William J.	Cannons Mill	cpl	E
Millsack, Frederick G.	Lancaster, Penn.	pvt	E
Minick, Jesse H.	Bucyrus	pvt	A
Mish, Earl	Jeromesville	pvt	C
Mison, Eugene	Canton	pvt	F
* Mitchell, Charles	Canton	pvt	L
Mite, Raymond S.	East Liverpool	pvt	E
Moffett, Samuel L.	Mansfield	pvt	M
Mohn, Alva V.	Shreve	cpl	H
Mohn, John H.	Wadsworth	pvt	G
Mollenkopf, Louis	Bucyrus	pvt	A
Monastere, Arthur	Mansfield	pvt	M
Monnette, Ephraim G.	Bucyrus	cpl	A
Moon, Samuel	East Liverpool	pvt	E
Moore, John James	Bucyrus	pvt	A
Moore, Murray D.	Alliance	pvt	K
Moore, Philip	East Liverpool	pvt	E
Moreland, Harvey C.	Canton	cpl	L
Morlan, Beecher	East Liverpool	pvt	E
Morley, Edwin S.	East Liverpool	cpl	E
Morris, John M.	Alliance	pvt	K, hq
Morris, Walter	Akron	pvt	B
Morrison, Herbert	Shreve	cpl	H
Morrison, Joseph Clyde	Akron	cpl	B
Morrow, Harry W.	Bucyrus	pvt	A
Moseley, Howard J.	Wooster	pvt	D
Moser, David F.	Mansfield	pvt	M
Mossgrove, Oliver P.	Canton	pvt	L
Moyer, Lloyd F.	Alliance	sgt	K
Mumaw, John H.	Canton	pvt	I
Mumaw, Welker A.	Canton	pvt	I
Munz, Frank	Bucyrus	pvt	A
Murphy, Marion M.	Canton	cpl	I
Murray, John W.	East Liverpool	pvt	E
Mushrush, Ira G.	Toronto	pvt	E
Myers, John P.	Wooster	pvt	D
Myers, Ralph H.	Mansfield	pvt	M
Myers, Walter W.	Canton	pvt	F
Myers, William W.	Canton	pvt	F

* died

	Name	Home	Rank	Company
	Naftzger, Lloyd A.	Wooster	wagoner	D
*	Naftzger, Vernon R.	Wooster	pvt	D
	Nail, Charles	Bucyrus	pvt	A
	Nause, William W.	Alliance	pvt	K
	Nedele, Lewis S.	Bucyrus	sgt	A
	Neiswanger, Ellis B.	Orrville	pvt	H
*	Nelson, Arthur	Akron	pvt	B
	Nelson, Frank	Akron	pvt	B
	Nelson, Samuel H.	Bucyrus	pvt	A
	Neubert, Conrad	Mansfield	pvt	M
	Newcomer, Jesse	Alliance	pvt	K
	Newcomer, William H.	Canton	pvt	L
	Newhouse, John Alfred	Canton	pvt	L
	Newton, John	Fredericksburg	pvt	C
	Nicely, Arthur H.	Wadsworth	pvt	G
	Nichols, Arthur J.	Mansfield	pvt	M
	Nieschwitz, Charles	Canton	pvt	F
	Niswender, Carl W.	Wadsworth	pvt	G
	Nixon, Ralph K.	Canton	pvt	I
	Nolan, David H.	Nova	cpl	C
	Nolan, Frank J.	Nova	cpl	C
	Norris, Willis W.	Wooster	pvt	D
	Oberholser, William J.	Akron	pvt	K, hq
	Ogline, Edward	Alliance	pvt	K
	Olinger, Edward	Canton	pvt	F
	Oltmanns, Antoni	Wooster	pvt	D
	O'Mara, Patrick J.	Wadsworth	pvt	G
	Oppenheimer, Otto J.	Canton	hosp steward	hq
	O'Rourke, John H.	East Liverpool	pvt	E
	Orr, Benjamin L.	Bucyrus	pvt	A
	Orr, William R.	Bucyrus	pvt	A
	Ortt, Otis	Canton	pvt	F
	Osborn, Bert R.	Alliance	pvt	K
	Oschman, Edward J.	East Liverpool	pvt	F
	Oschmann, Fred G.	East Liverpool	pvt	E
	Outland, William C.	Akron	pvt	B
	Overholt, Charles H.	Wadsworth	pvt	G
	Overholt, Frank C.	Mansfield	pvt	M
	Overholt, George	Seville	pvt	G

* died

NAME	HOME	RANK	COMPANY
Paisley, George S.	East Liverpool	pvt	L
Paisley, William L.	East Liverpool	pvt	E
Palmer, William R.	Akron	chief musician	hq
Patterson, Jay H.	Ashland	pvt	C
* Patterson, John O.	Alliance	pvt	K
Patterson, Thomas C.	Killbuck	pvt	H
Penfield, Ernest	Canton	pvt	F
Pennock, Frederick R.	Canton	pvt	L
Pfirman, Franklin	Canton	pvt	F, hosp
Philips, Charles Lee	Camp Alger, Va.	pvt	I
Phipps, Elda L.	Mansfield	pvt	M
Piero, Oliver J.	Canton	pvt	I
Pinnicks, Sinclair J.	Wooster	pvt	D
Plank, Harry F.	Wooster	pvt	D
Plank, Joshua M.	Ashland	pvt	C
Plum, Floyd H.	Wooster	pvt	D
Plummer, Thomas	Bucyrus	pvt	A
Pool, Lewis M.	East Liverpool	pvt	E
Porch, Roscoe E.	Mansfield	cpl	M
Ports, Delbert A.	Clark	pvt	H
Ports, Harry A.	Clark	pvt	H
Post, Ira E.	Mansfield	pvt	M
Potts, Bert	Canton	pvt	F
Potts, Robert	East Liverpool	pvt	E
Prendeville, James P.	Canton	pvt	F
Price, John H.	Alliance	pvt	K
Prien, Otis E.	Akron	sgt	B
Prior, George A.	Akron	pvt	B
Provines, James	Canton	pvt	I
Pruden, Charles E.	Canton	wagoner	L
Pruner, Willis G.	Medina	pvt	G
Pugh, Edward H.	Mansfield	pvt	M
Pumphrey, Ernest M.	Canton	pvt	L
Purdy, Charles O.	Holmesville	pvt	H
Purinton, Charles A.	East Liverpool	sgt	E
Purnell, Lew E.	Canton	pvt	F
Putnam, Edwin P.	Medina	pvt	G

* died

NAME	HOME	RANK	COMPANY
Quaill, Theodore L.	Canton	pvt	I
Query, Deward	Hayesville	pvt	C
Quine, Harry S.	Akron	cpl	B
Raber, Ernest L.	Canton	cpl	F
Rabon, James D.	East Liverpool	pvt	E
Ralston, Robert J.	Canton	pvt	L
Raub, Charles W.	Bucyrus	musician	A
Rayel, T. P.	Bucyrus	pvt	A
Raymond, Samuel F.	Bucyrus	cpl	A
Rea, Charles T.	Canton	cpl	I
Rea, George	Canton	batt sgt maj	I, hq
Rebaux, Curtis A.	Akron	pvt	G
Reber, William F.	Bucyrus	cpl	A
* Redding, Frank	Ashland	pvt	C
Redman, Charles F.	Canton	pvt	I
Reed, William F.	Canton	pvt	L
Reed, William W.	Mansfield	pvt	M
Reid, Edward G.	Bucyrus	batt sgt maj	hq
Reimensnyder, Charles C.	Canton	pvt	L
Reinert, Charles	Akron	pvt	B
Reininger, Theodore	Bucyrus	pvt	A
Renie, George	Canton	pvt	L
Reniker, Alfred W.	East Liverpool	pvt	E
Renn, John Z.	Ashland	pvt	C
Renner, Edward C.	Canton	cpl	I
Renny, Richard W.	Canton	pvt	F
Rettig, Edward	Bucyrus	pvt	A
Rettig, John	Bucyrus	pvt	A
Reynolds, Aldene	Alliance	musician	K
Reynolds, Delran C.	East Liverpool	pvt	F
Reynolds, Eugene	Alliance	pvt	K
Reynolds, Frank	Bucyrus	pvt	A
Reynolds, Oliver C.	East Liverpool	pvt	E
Rice, Orlando C.	Bucyrus	pvt	A
Rich, Elmer	Canton	pvt	L
Richards, Joseph E.	Alliance	pvt	K
Richards, Martin A.	Alliance	pvt	K
Richardson, Maurice	Hinckley	pvt	G

* died

NAME	HOME	RANK	COMPANY
Richter, William P.	Akron	pvt	B, deserted
Ricket, Orlo J.	Sullivan	pvt	C
Rickets, Richard H.	Mansfield	pvt	M
Rider, William H.	Alliance	pvt	K
Ridgley, Roy	Ashland	pvt	C
Rieder, Edmond S.	Wooster	pvt	D
Riffle, Albert E.	Wooster	pvt	H
Ringle, Homer G.	Canton	cpl	I
Rittenhouse, Emmet C.	Ashland	pvt	C
Ritter, William A.	Akron	pvt	B
Roberts, Edward E.	East Liverpool	pvt	L
Roberts, John	Akron	pvt	B
Robertson, Alexander	Alliance	pvt	K
Robertson, William W.	Wooster	pvt	D
Robinett, William L.	Mount Hope	pvt	H
Robinson, Edson M.	Akron	pvt	B
Robinson, John	East Liverpool	pvt	E
Robinson, John E.	Canton	cpl	F
Robinson, Louis J.	Ashland	pvt	C
Robison, Bert D.	Shreve	sgt	H
Robison, Marion S.	Shreve	2d lt	H
Robison, Walter	Shreve	pvt	H
Robusch, John	Alliance	pvt	K
Rodey, Edward	Bucyrus	1st sgt	A
Roethlisberger, Urich	Mansfield	pvt	M
Rogers, Arthur C.	Canton	musician	L
Rogers, Birt	Bucyrus	pvt	A
Rogers, George W.	Akron	cpl	B
Rohleder, David T.	Ashland	pvt	G
Rohrer, John S.	Canton	pvt	K
Rood, Luther W.	Akron	pvt	B
* Roos, John	Akron	pvt	B
Rope, John W.	Wooster	pvt	H
Roshon, Charles A.	Medina	pvt	G
Roshong, Harry L.	Canton	pvt	L
Ross, Amos L.	Wooster	pvt	D
Roussert, Albert	Akron	musician	B
Royer, Charles S.	New Baltimore	pvt	K
* Royer, Ora N.	Alliance	pvt	K
Rubin, Christian	Canton	pvt	F

* died

Name	Home	Rank	Company
Russell, Albert M.	Canton	musician	I
Rutherford, William O.	Akron	2d lt	B
Ruttman, Daniel W.	Akron	pvt	B, hq
Saeger, Roy S.	Canton	sgt	I
Sample, Herbert L.	Canton	pvt	I
Sampsel, Sherman	Bucyrus	pvt	A
* Sandhammer, Otto	Bucyrus	pvt	A
Saner, Bert M.	Cedar Rapids, Iowa	pvt	G
Santrock, Frederick W.	Doylestown	wagoner	G
Sattler, Thomas O.	Ashland	pvt	C
Sawhill, Edward J.	Mansfield	pvt	M
Scanlain, Thomas	New Haven, Conn.	pvt	C
Schaber, Charles F.	Bucyrus	2d lt	hq
Schaffer, Robert C.	Alliance	pvt	K
Schaffer, William H.	Alliance	pvt	K
Schauweker, James T.	Canton	pvt	I
Schicker, Frank P.	Canton	cpl	F
Schodorf, George A.	Berlin	pvt	H
Schopf, William F.	Ashland	pvt	C
Schott, Wilfred B.	West Salem	pvt	C
Schuch, Fred A.	Wooster	pvt	D
Schuck, William	Wooster	pvt	D
Schumacher, Fred W.	Canton	pvt	I
Scott, Charles W.	Alliance	cpl	K
Scott, Charlie R.	Wooster	cpl	D
Scott, Harry H.	Canton	pvt	L
Scott, John M.	Alliance	pvt	K
Scott, Thomas J.	Alliance	pvt	K
Seacrist, Edd	Alliance	pvt	K
Seacrist, Elwood E.	Alliance	pvt	K
Secrest, Charles B.	East Liverpool	pvt	E
Seeger, Lucius E. D.	Canton	cpl	I
Seese, Dorsey	Canton	pvt	L
Seevers, Noah C.	East Liverpool	pvt	E
Segner, Robert, Jr.	Wooster	pvt	D
Seib, William	Funk	pvt	H
Seikel, Frank A.	Canton	pvt	L
Seiler, George	Akron	pvt	G

* died

NAME	HOME	RANK	COMPANY
Semler, Daniel H.	Canton	pvt	L
Serfass, Charles R.	Akron	cpl	B
Sexton, William W.	Canton	pvt	F
Seymour, Joseph D.	Mansfield	pvt	M
Shade, Warner S.	Mansfield	pvt	M
Shaffer, Arthur O.	Medina	pvt	G
Shaffer, Ira J.	Alliance	pvt	K
Shaffer, Lyman E.	Akron	pvt	B
Shanks, Charles E.	Bucyrus	pvt	A
Sharp, Richard A.	Canton	pvt	L
Shea, Charles E.	Mansfield	pvt	M
Sheaffer, Robert H.	Canton	pvt	F
* Sheets, Byron A.	Rittman	pvt	G
Sheldon, George T.	Canton	pvt	I
Shepherd, William M.	East Liverpool	pvt	E
Sherry, Clifford E.	Canton	pvt	L
Shew, Orrin P.	Canton	pvt	I
Shew, Samuel J.	Canton	pvt	I
Shine, Francis M.	Canton	pvt	I
Shotts, Charles E.	Canton	pvt	F
Shrader, Samuel	Mansfield	pvt	M
Shriver, Charles E.	Canton	pvt	F
Shroyer, John W.	Canton	pvt	F
Shumacher, Frank	Wadsworth	pvt	G
Siegfried, John J.	Wadsworth	pvt	G
Silver, Edwin B.	Alliance	sgt	K
Silver, James A.	Alliance	cpl	K
Simms, Ezra H.	East Liverpool	pvt	E
Simon, John T.	Mansfield	pvt	M
* Simpson, Amos G.	Mansfield	pvt	M
Simpson, Charles H.	Canton	pvt	L
Skeels, Walter E.	Canton	pvt	F
Skelly, Alfred M.	Holmesville	cpl	H
Sliker, Harry W.	Canton	pvt	I
Slusser, Lincoln A.	Canton	cpl	L
Smart, Herbert C.	Canton	2d lt	L
Smith, Allen V.	Canton	capt and asst surg	hq
Smith, Anson H.	Mansfield	wagoner	M
Smith, Edgar	Wadsworth	pvt	G

* died

	Name	Home	Rank	Company
*	Smith, Francis	East Liverpool	pvt	E
	Smith, Frederick A.	East Liverpool	pvt	E
	Smith, George A.	East Liverpool	pvt	E
	Smith, George F.	Akron	pvt	B
	Smith, Harry A.	East Liverpool	pvt	E
	Smith, Harry E.	East Liverpool	pvt	E
	Smith, John	Canton	pvt	F
	Smith, John H.	Canton	cpl	F
	Smith, Lewis A.	Ashland	pvt	C
	Smith, Olin Lee	Wooster	pvt	D
	Smith, Thomas C.	East Liverpool	sgt	E
	Smith, Vernon J.	Wooster	pvt	D
	Smith, William F.	Shreve	pvt	H
	Snoddy, Allen C.	Albion	pvt	C
	Snyder, Charles A.	Akron	pvt	B
	Snyder, Ernest	Akron	pvt	G, deserted
	Snyder, John	Canton	pvt	F
	Snyder, Joseph C.	Canton	cpl	L
	Snyder, Milo D.	Akron	musician	G, hq
	Snyder, Norman R.	Mansfield	pvt	M
	Snyder, Samuel	Akron	pvt	G
	Sonnanstine, Walter G.	Wadsworth	pvt	G
	Souers, James E. F.	Akron	pvt	B
	Sourbeck, Alva L.	Alliance	pvt	K
*	Spade, Charles A.	Akron	pvt	B
	Spade, Daniel	Bucyrus	cook	A
	Spafford, Willis B.	Akron	pvt	B
	Spangler, Charles	Canton	pvt	I
	Spangler, John A.	Canton	pvt	I
	Spencer, John E.	Sullivan	cpl	C
	Spencer, William A.	Akron	pvt	B
	Spidel, Herbert S.	Canton	1st lt	F
*	Spitler, Durban W.	Mansfield	cpl	M
	Spotts, Hugh J.	Canton	cpl	I
	Spotts, Ralph L.	Canton	1st sgt	I
	Sprague, Arthur E.	Akron	pvt	B
	Stahl, Frederick	Bucyrus	pvt	A
	Stailey, Milton	Bucyrus	sgt	A
	Stair, Blaine A.	Akron	pvt	B
	Stands, Frank J.	Canton	pvt	L

* died

	Name	Home	Rank	Company
	Stanley, Edgar A.	Bucyrus	pvt	A
	Starrett, Jesse A.	Mansfield	sgt	M
	Stauffer, Abraham L.	Wadsworth	cpl	G
	Steadman, Harry K.	Akron	pvt	F, hq
	Steitz, Lewis	Canton	pvt	I
	Stephens, Leroy	Alliance	pvt	K
	Stevens, Thomas R.	Wooster	cpl	D
	Stewart, Harry	Millersburg	pvt	H
	Stewart, Ralph J.	Bucyrus	pvt	A
	Stine, Albert M.	East Liverpool	pvt	E
	Stoffel, Clyde V.	East Liverpool	pvt	E
	Stokey, Fred E.	Canton	pvt	K
	Stoll, Oscar L.	Mansfield	pvt	M
	Stormfeltz, Charles C.	Canton	pvt	F
	Stotsbery, Charles C.	Wooster	pvt	D
	Stotsbery, John F.	Wooster	pvt	D
	Stotsbery, William A.	Wooster	pvt	D
	Strachan, Robert	Wadsworth	pvt	G
	Streby, Edward	Canton	pvt	F
*	Strobel, Edward B.	Akron	pvt	B
*	Struggles, Willis Clark	Wadsworth	hosp steward	hq
	Stuber, George W.	Millersburg	pvt	H
	Stump, John A.	Canton	pvt	L
	Sullivan, Michael L.	Alliance	cpl	K
	Summerville, Carl B.	Mansfield	pvt	M
	Suter, George	Canton	pvt	L
	Swarts, George M.	Wooster	cpl	D
	Swarts, John T.	Wooster	pvt	D
	Swarts, Stanford M.	Shreve	1st lt	H
	Swartz, William B.	Wooster	pvt	D
	Sweringen, Frank	Ashland	pvt	C
	Swift, Oliver H.	Akron	pvt	B
	Swineford, Harry	Ashland	pvt	C
	Swingly, Guy D.	Bucyrus	2d lt	A
	Swingwood, George	East Liverpool	pvt	E
*	Switzer, Charles W.	East Liverpool	pvt	E
	Switzer, David O.	Holmesville	pvt	H

* died

	Name	Home	Rank	Company
	Tallon, Bernard	Ashland	pvt	C
	Tanner, Wilbur J.	Creston	pvt	G
	Tanneyhill, Franklin	Akron	cpl	B
	Tarleton, Clare C.	Canton	pvt	I
*	Tarner, Charles E.	Canton	cpl	L
	Taylor, Frank H.	Canton	pvt	I
	Taylor, John E.	Steubenville	pvt	E
	Taylor, Kaiser W.	Polk	1st lt	C
	Taylor, Robert N.	Carrollton	pvt	E
	Taylor, Roscoe A.	Bucyrus	pvt	A
	Taylor, Thomas E.	Mansfield	pvt	M
	Taylor, Ulysses S.	Akron	pvt	G
	Tebay, Warren W.	Canton	pvt	I
	Teeple, Arthur R.	Akron	pvt	B
	Teeterick, Albert	Bucyrus	pvt	A
	Teeters, Carl D.	Alliance	pvt	E
	Terrett, Edward P.	Canton	1st sgt	I
*	Thoman, Charles J.	Bucyrus	sgt	A
	Thoman, William B.	Canton	pvt	L
	Thomas, David R.	Akron	pvt	B
	Thomas, James R.	Akron	sgt	B
	Thomen, Edward C.	Wooster	pvt	D
*	Thompson, Otis P.	Medina	pvt	G
	Thurin, George A.	Canton	pvt	L
	Tobin, Joseph P.	Canton	pvt	L
	Trautman, Frank	Bucyrus	pvt	A
	Treap, Harry F.	Akron	sgt	B
	Trease, Davis	Mansfield	pvt	M
	Trescott, Ernest	Alliance	wagoner	K
*	Treuthardt, John G.	Alliance	pvt	K
	Trover, William C.	East Liverpool	pvt	E
	Trumbull, Roscoe A.	Bucyrus	pvt	A
	Trump, Frank L.	East Liverpool	qm sgt	E
	Tucker, Charles S.	Mansfield	pvt	M
	Tucker, William D.	Canton	pvt	F
	Tuttle, Harry G.	Creston	pvt	G

* died

NAME	HOME	RANK	COMPANY
Uebelhart, Nicholas	Canton	pvt	L
Uebelhart, William J.	Alliance	pvt	K, hosp
Ullom, Bert	Bucyrus	pvt	A
Ungashick, Frank A.	Canton	cpl	I
Unger, Charles E.	Wooster	cpl	D
Unger, Gustave W.	Wooster	2d lt	D
Urig, Edmund J.	Alliance	pvt	K
Van Dervort, Carl R.	Canton	pvt	F
Van Epp, Arthur	Medina	pvt	G
Vernosky, John	Akron	pvt	G
Vogelsang, Alfred L.	Canton	artificer	I
Vogelsang, Elmer J.	Canton	pvt	L
Volk, Henry E.	Bucyrus	cpl	A
Vollrath, Edward	Bucyrus	maj	hq
Wagner, Edwin S.	Canton	cpl	F
Wagner, Frank L.	Canton	pvt	I, hosp
Wagoner, Mason L.	Canton	pvt	I
Wait, Ralph H.	Weymouth	pvt	G
Walcutt, Bert J.	Canton	pvt	F
Walker, James A. G.	Canton	musician	L, hq
Walker, Otis U.	Alliance	pvt	K
Walker, Tony S.	Alliance	pvt	K
Walkup, Royal A.	Akron	cpl	B
Walkup, William E.	Akron	1st sgt	B
Walser, Richard	Alliance	pvt	K
Walsh, Michael	Canton	pvt	F
Ward, James E.	East Liverpool	pvt	E
Warden, Albert E.	Bucyrus	pvt	A
Warner, Charles E.	Pleasant Home	cpl	C
Warner, Clare R.	Medina	pvt	G
Warner, John H.	Canton	cpl	L
Warner, John J.	Mansfield	pvt	M
Warner, Joy W.	Mansfield	pvt	M
Warrell, Thomas J.	Mansfield	pvt	M
Way, Charles	Ashland	pvt	C
Way, Elbert Wesley	Paint Valley	pvt	H
Weaver, Allen	Wadsworth	sgt	G
Weaver, Charles	Shreve	pvt	H
Weaver, Samuel E.	Wooster	pvt	D

	Name	Home	Rank	Company
	Weaver, Vaughn P.	East Liverpool	cpl	E
	Webb, George B.	Wooster	pvt	D
	Weber, Andrew	Mansfield	pvt	M
	Weidman, August	Canton	capt	F
	Weidman, George	Canton	sgt	F
*	Weiker, Leonard L.	Shreve	artificer	H
	Weisen, Mike	Wadsworth	pvt	G
	Weiss, Raymond	Akron	pvt	B
	Wells, Clarence	Creston	pvt	G
	Wells, William J.	Wadsworth	sgt	G
	Welty, Clement J.	Wadsworth	pvt	C
	Wert, Joseph E.	Bucyrus	qm sgt	A
	Wertenberger, William H.	Canton	pvt	L
	Wertman, Charles A.	Ashland	pvt	C
	Wertman, Edd	Ashland	pvt	C
	Wetzel, John	Akron	pvt	B
	Weybrecht, Andrew T.	Alliance	2d lt and batt adj	hq
	Weybrecht, Charles C.	Alliance	maj	hq
	Whalen, George	Akron	pvt	B
	Wheeler, Walter R.	Akron	pvt	B
	Whipple, John L.	Canton	qm sgt	I
	White, Charles	Shreve	pvt	H
	White, Charles L.	Alliance	cpl	K
	White, George Homer	Canton	wagoner	F
	White, Harry B.	Millersburg	cpl	H
	Whiteman, Walter L.	Canton	pvt	I
	Whiteman, William H.	Mansfield	pvt	M
	Whitestine, David	Akron	wagoner	B
	Wiley, Charles O.	Alliance	cpl	K
*	Wilford, Ward A.	Akron	pvt	B
	Wilkinson, George A.	East Liverpool	pvt	E
	Wilkinson, Paul	Canton	pvt	F
	Willaman, Clement H.	Canton	pvt	F
	Williams, Idris C.	Akron	pvt	B
	Williams, Timothy	East Liverpool	pvt	E
	Williamson, Samuel	Toronto	pvt	E
*	Willis, Henry L.	Canton	capt	I
*	Wilson, Dudley D.	River Styx	cpl	G

* died

	NAME	HOME	RANK	COMPANY
	Wilson, Jay B.	Jeromesville	cpl	C
	Wilson, William D.	Steubenville	pvt	E
	Winebrenner, Calvin A.	Wooster	pvt	D
	Wingard, John L.	Canton	pvt	L
*	Wingerter, Edward S.	Canton	pvt	I
	Winner, Harry R.	Bucyrus	pvt	A
	Winters, Edward H.	Mansfield	pvt	M
	Winters, George E.	Canton	cpl	L
	Winters, Harry H.	Canton	pvt	L
	Wise, Edward M.	Bucyrus	cpl	A
	Wise, Homer A.	Canton	sgt, 2d lt	I
	Wise, Tilden	Redhaw	pvt	C
	Wise, Warren S. C.	Canton	pvt	L
	Witt, Louis G.	Canton	pvt	I
	Witter, Charles A.	Canton	cpl	I
	Woehler, Henry C.	Akron	pvt	A, hq
	Wolfe, Charles	Ashland	pvt	C
	Wolff, Wiliam B.	Mansfield	pvt	M
	Wollweber, Otto	Bucyrus	principal musician	hq
	Wood, Ralph A.	East Liverpool	cpl	E
	Woods, Frank F.	Akron	pvt	B
	Woods, William	Ashland	pvt	C
	Woolman, Harry D.	Wooster	cpl	D
	Worthington, Elmer A.	Akron	pvt	G
	Worthington, William W.	Akron	musician	C, hq
	Wright, George M.	Akron	2d lt and batt adj	hq
	Wuchter, George H.	Wadsworth	capt and asst surg	hq
	Wyman, George E.	East Liverpool	cpl	E
	Wyre, Orphanas F.	Millbrook	pvt	H
	Wyre, Sherman Z.	Millbrook	pvt	H
	Yoder, Archie L.	Wadsworth	pvt	G
	Yoder, Charles J.	Wadsworth	pvt	G
	Yoder, Claude L.	Wadsworth	cpl	G
	Yoder, Ephraim S.	Wooster	pvt	D
	Yoder, Harvey O.	Wadsworth	qm sgt	G

---

* died

NAME	HOME	RANK	COMPANY
Yohey, George E.	Akron	pvt	B, hq
Yost, Philip	Canton	capt	I
Yost, William E.	Canton	pvt	I
Young, Charles R.	Mansfield	pvt	M
Young, John A.	Canton	artificer	L
Young, John J.	Canton	pvt	F
Young, Joseph S.	Canton	pvt	L
Young, Joseph W.	Akron	sgt maj, 2d lt	F, hq
Zang, Fred J.	Alliance	pvt	K
Zerbe, Perry	Canton	pvt	F, hq
Ziegler, Louis C.	Savannah	pvt	C
Zimmerman, Gustav	Canton	pvt	L
Zimmerman, Harry P.	Alliance	pvt	K
Zuber, Charles H.	Alliance	pvt	K
Zuber, George A.	Alliance	musician	K

* died

Notes

I Mobilization

1. Crouse was a prominent Akron industrialist and Civil War veteran, who lent money to Dr. B.F. Goodrich to start the first rubber plant, and rescued it by endorsing promissory notes up to $45,000 in 1878, for which he received one fifth of the company's stock. He was one of the owners of the *Akron Beacon*. William E. Young, a lawyer, served as mayor of Akron from 1896 to 1900. His tenure was marked by the burning of city hall by a mob, during his last year in office. Wagoner, a veteran of the Civil War, was an Akron banker. Frank M. Atterholt was a prominent lawyer. Edward A. Hershey was clerk of the court of common pleas. Dr. Ebright in 1895 had gone to Cleveland during an outbreak of diphtheria and brought back enough serum for seventy children of the Children's Home. Dr. Lewis E. Sisler was a physician, had served as county auditor, and was one of the founders of the Firestone Tire and Rubber Company; he was secretary and later treasurer and director of the company. Judge George M. Anderson presided over probate court. Paul E. Werner was a notable citizen of Akron. Born in Germany in 1850, emigrating in 1867, he became head of the largest book-printing company in the United States. Among other activities he printed the *Encyclopaedia Britannica*. His company went into bankruptcy in 1909 and again in 1914, and his opposition to American entry into World War I made recovery difficult. In an attempt to reestablish himself he removed to Kansas City. He returned to Akron in 1926 and died in 1931. (Good sources for turn-of-the-century biographies are Samuel Alanson Lane, *Fifty Years and Over of Akron and Summit County* (Akron, 1892), and Karl H. Grismer, *Akron and Summit County* (Akron: Summit County Historical Society, [1952?]).

2. Jacob A. Kohler was judge of common pleas. Newell D. Tibballs had been judge in 1876-83.

3. James B. Taylor was a Civil War veteran and lawyer.

4. Charles W. F. Dick was born in 1858 at Akron of German-American parents. He was elected auditor of Summit County in 1886 and was admitted to the bar in 1894. Meanwhile, in 1892, he had become chairman of the Ohio Republican state convention, and from 1896 until 1900 served as secretary of the Chicago headquarters of the Republican National Committee. During the Spanish-American War he continued to receive his salary of one hundred dollars a week from the National Committee. He was elected to Congress in 1898, and in the House of Representatives became author of the Dick Militia Act of 1903, which wrote into law the federal

recognition of and aid to the National Guard. Appointed to the Senate in 1904, elected in November of that year, he failed to be re-elected in 1910. His papers are in the Ohio Historical Society.

5. The horses of the Eighth did not accompany the regiment to Cuba. "The horses belonging to our officers, thirteen in number, could not be loaded on the *St. Paul*, but were put aboard another ship, together with the horses of the other two regiments of our brigade. Up to August 14 we never heard of them, and presumed they had been lost. Great was our surprise on that morning to learn that they were in Santiago harbor, after having been taken to Puerto Rico and used in that campaign. All of them were in fairly good condition, and we brought them home with us, and have them now." Capt. Herman L. Kuhns, "Feeding an Army," pt. 6, *Hotel World*, clippings in Dudley Hard Papers, Western Reserve Historical Society, Cleveland.

II Washington

1. The camp was named after Secretary of War Russell A. Alger. Born in 1836, probably a distant relative of the well-known author of boys' success stories, a veteran of the Civil War, one-term (1885-87) governor of Michigan, wealthy lumberman, Alger was a sensible if emotional man, much concerned for the welfare of the common soldier—he visited the Eighth Ohio at Camp Wikoff after the war. The focus of much public criticism of mobilization and conduct of the war, he became a political liability, and President McKinley in 1899 replaced him with the New York lawyer Elihu Root. Alger was elected to the Senate from Michigan in 1902 and served until his death in 1907. For the conventional view of Alger as a goateed fuddy-duddy, see Frederic Logan Paxton's sketch in the *Dictionary of American Biography*, s.v. "Alger, Russell A." A more balanced judgment is in Graham Cosmas, *An Army for Empire: The United States Army in the Spanish-American War* (Columbia, Mo.: Univ. of Missouri Press, 1971), pp. 55–58.

2. Born in 1834, William M. Graham had entered the Regular Army in 1855 and served in the Civil War in the Peninsular Campaign and at Gettysburg. In postwar years he took part in an Indian campaign and rose in rank to brigadier general in 1897. Appointed major general of volunteers during the Spanish-American War, he retired immediately afterward. He died in 1916. *DAB*, s.v. "William Montrose Graham." Matthew C. Butler was born two years after General Graham, in 1836. His mother was the sister of Commodores Oliver Hazard and Matthew C. Perry. He was the eleventh of sixteen children. He entered the Confederate Army at the outset of the Civil War, and lost his right foot at the Battle of Brandy Station—not far from the Camp Alger of 1898. He represented South Carolina for three terms in the Senate, until defeat by Benjamin R. (Pitchfork Ben) Tillman in 1894. Appointed major general of volunteers in 1898, he afterward served as a member of the commission for the Spanish evacuation of Cuba. He died in Washington in 1906. *DAB*, s.v. "Matthew Calbraith Butler."

3. Brig. Gen. Garretson received a command in the Puerto Rican expedition. A graduate of West Point in 1867, he resigned from the army in 1870 and spent his life as a banker in Cleveland, dying in 1916. His papers are in the Western Reserve Historical Society.

4. Col. Hard was very proud of the Eighth Ohio's band, and believed it to be "the finest in the camp." Under the direction of chief musician William R. Palmer, it easily put other military bands to shame, especially those of the Regular Army, in which a bandsman's pay was $13 a month. Palmer had organized his band in Akron, and during the presidential campaign of 1896 it had accompanied McKinley on trips. When war broke out it had been part of the Eighth for nearly twenty years, and even though the enlistment period for two-thirds of the regiment's

musicians expired that month, the band, in Palmer's words, "decided to share the experience of war with them." See the excellent article by Palmer's grand-niece, Priscilla M. Harding, "McKinley's Own: An Ohio Band Plays the 'Splendid Little War,'" *Timeline* 2 (Oct.-Nov. 1985): 10–21.

5. According to Orders 30 of the Eighth, Camp Alger, May 25, regimental routine was as follows: 5:15 first call for Reveille; 5:30 Reveille and Assembly; 5:45 breakfast; 6:15 general police of camp; 6:30 drill (School of Soldier); 7:30 Recall; 8:00–9:00 theoretical instructions; 9:30 drill (School of Company); 11:00 Recall; 12:00 dinner; 1:30 guard mounting; 2:00–2:30 theoretical instruction; 3:00 drill (School Battalion); 4:30 Recall; 5:30 supper; 6:30 parade; 9:00 call to quarters; 9:30 Taps. Regimental records, vol. 2, Record Group 94, National Archives, Washington, D.C.

6. The "rookie" dress parade was a notable occasion, what with almost four hundred men dressed in grotesque costumes. Led by the band, they marched the opposite of usual ways. They carefully burlesqued Col. Hard and staff, whose replicas appeared with paper shoulder straps and medals.

III Getting Ready

1. Hard kept the president informed about the McKinley relatives. His first letter related that he had enlisted James McKinley in Company I. Hard to McKinley, June 23, 1898, McKinley MSS, Library of Congress, microfilm, series 1, reel 3. After the regiment reached Cuba the president cabled about them, and Hard responded that they had landed July 10, two days later were detailed as orderlies to Brig. Gen. Guy V. Henry who had gone back aboard a transport, and that they had been well when they left the Eighth. Eventually they accompanied Henry to Puerto Rico. Hard to McKinley, letter of July 25, telegram of Aug. 8, McKinley MSS, microfilm, series 1, reel 4.

2. Burton had been the *Washington Post*'s correspondent at Camp Alger.

3. Capt. Kuhns of Canton afterward wrote a seven-part account of "Feeding an Army," for *Hotel World*, a magazine published in New York and Chicago, and evidently sent a copy to Col. Hard, whose papers contain all parts except the first.

4. Born in 1830, Oliver O. Howard graduated from West Point in 1854 and during the Civil War rose to the rank of brigadier general in the Regular Army. His service in the war was prominent but he was often criticized for poor judgment. After the war he took charge of the Freedmen's Bureau and again received much criticism, some of it undoubtedly partisan. He founded Howard University in Washington and became its president in 1869, resigning in 1874. He commanded the expedition against the Nez Perce under Chief Joseph in 1877. Promoted to major general in 1886, he retired in 1894 and died in 1909. *DAB*, s.v. "Oliver Otis Howard."

5. Secretary Alger told Col. Hard that "There is not a man in your regiment but can read and write, and yours is the first muster roll of that description we have received." Manuscript of Hard memoir. The secretary, however, was wrong, for George W. Campbell of Company E signed the roll with an "X." See regimental records in the National Archives, vol. 4, RG 94.

6. In his manuscript memoir Hard names some of his visitors—Senator Hanna, Messrs. Chen and Chow of the Chinese legation, Senator Joseph B. Foraker of Ohio, the journalist Murat Halstead, and Clara Barton.

7. Hard had received a letter from one of the eight survivors resident in Washington that began: "I have been requested by the resident members of the 8th Ohio Vol. Inf. War of 1861 to 5, to notify you that we will visit your camp on Sunday afternoon 12th inst. on or about 3:30 o'clock." Hard manuscript memoir.

8. $15.60 per month.

IV Aboard the *St. Paul*

1. Charles D. Sigsbee was a well-known officer at the time of the war with Spain, having been captain of the ill-fated *Maine*. Born in Albany, he graduated from the Naval Academy in 1863. He participated in the Battle of Mobile Bay the next year, and after transfer to the North Atlantic blockading squadron took part in both attacks on Fort Fisher. After duty with the Asiatic Squadron he returned to teach at the academy, and had three tours there. In 1875-78 he commanded the Coast Survey steamer *Blake*, engaging in deep-sea exploration, principally in the Gulf of Mexico, for which he made a complete deep-water survey. In recognition of this work its deepest area was named Sigsbee Deep. He received command of the *Maine* in 1897. Afterward, he took command of the *St. Paul*, and on May 25 captured the British collier *Restormel*, laden with coal for the squadron of Admiral Pascual Cervera y Topete. On June 22 he engaged and defeated a Spanish destroyer, the *Terror*, and a cruiser, the *Isabella II*, off San Juan, Puerto Rico. After the war he was advanced three numbers in rank for "extraordinary heroism." Promoted to rear admiral in 1903, he received the task in 1905 of sailing to Cherbourg and bringing back the body of John Paul Jones for reburial at the Naval Academy. He retired in 1907, and died in 1923. *DAB*, s.v. "Charles Dwight Sigsbee." During the voyage to Santiago, Brig. Gen. Adelbert Ames (see below, note 3) elicited some testimony from Sigsbee about the *Maine*: "Capt. Sigsbee is a good talker and is most interesting in his accounts of the incidents connected with the destruction of the *Maine*. . . . He does not give his opinions as to who did the deed, tho' he has them. He says he told our authorities how the torpedo could be placed 'right under our eyes and I not know it.' As he has no proof he can not afford to pass sentence on anyone." Ames diary, July 7, 1898, U.S. Army Military History Institute Archives, Carlisle Barracks, Penn.

2. Sigsbee was anxious to sail, as New York harbor had been mined and daylight was necessary to pilot ships out of port. Capt. Kuhns wrote that no ship ordinarily left after 6:00 P.M., and that the *St. Paul* departed at 7:00 under a special dispensation. "Feeding an Army," pts. 1 and 4, *Hotel World*.

3. Brig. Gen. Ames was born in 1835, graduated from West Point in 1861, and served in the campaigns of the Civil War, commanding a division at Gettysburg. He resigned from the army in 1870. During the years of Reconstruction he was both provisional and elected governor of Mississippi. He died in 1933. *DAB*, s.v. "Adelbert Ames," Supplement 1, 27–28. Ames's papers are in the Sophia Smith Collection, Smith College Archives, Northampton, Mass. Brig. Gen. Henry was born in 1839, graduated from West Point in 1861, and served through the Civil War and Indian campaigns, receiving several awards for gallantry. He died in 1899. Henry was a contemporary of Ames, and the latter's diary of the voyage to Cuba is replete with comments about Henry's gossip concerning American officers in Cuba, from Shafter on down. (But then Ames was something of a gossip, for he felt certain that Col. Hard and Lt. Col. Dick were President McKinley's representatives to the army in Cuba, sent down to check on Shafter.) James W. Wadsworth, born in 1846, served in the House of Representatives, 1881–85 and 1891–1907. He died in 1926.

4. During the loading of the *St. Paul* the Eighth's commissary officer, Capt. Kuhns, was busy, for he had to get aboard 15,000 lbs. of bacon, 10,014 lbs. of canned roast beef, 50,080 lbs. of hard bread, 12,250 lbs. of corned beef, 2,125 lbs. of beans, 5,400 lbs. of baked beans, 1,344 lbs. of rice, 44,808 lbs. of tomatoes, 2,625 lbs. of roasted coffee, 1,110 lbs. of roasted and ground coffee, 6,085 lbs. of sugar, 1,120 lbs. of salt, 138 lbs. of pepper, 1,206 lbs. of soap, 468 lbs. of candles, and 256 gals. of vinegar. "Feeding an Army," pt. 1, *Hotel World*.

5. For the men during the voyage there was no need to think they were on a pleasure trip, for ten or twelve were crowded into staterooms intended for four. Moreover, the electric fans

were shut off "and the rooms on the lower decks were exceedingly close and hot." Kuhns, "Feeding an Army," pt. 3, *Hotel World*.

6. William Randolph Hearst was owner of the *New York Journal*.

V Cuba

1. Here Col. Hard recalls an entry in the diary of Frederick W. Ramsden, British consul in Santiago, showing arrival of the *St. Paul*: "Tuesday, July 12, 1898: Rained heavily nearly all night and until noon today. General Miles has landed with more troops and six batteries of artillery and comes to the front this afternoon."

2. John Jacob Astor IV was born in 1864. A Harvard graduate, author of a semi-scientific novel entitled *A Journey in Other Worlds: A Romance of the Future* (New York: D. Appleton, 1894), manager of the family estate, in 1897 he supervised construction of the Astoria section of the old Waldorf-Astoria Hotel (torn down to make way for the Empire State Building during the 1920s; the name was transferred to a new hotel on Park Avenue). Commissioned lieutenant colonel of volunteers in 1898, he served on Gen. Shafter's staff. In later years he invented a bicycle brake and improved the turbine engine. He was drowned on the *Titanic* in 1912. *DAB*, s.v. "John Jacob Astor."

3. Calixto García was commander of insurgents in eastern Cuba, and had received messages from Americans before and during the landings asking that he harass the Spanish soldiery, and engage them until the Americans could establish beachheads. Leader of an ill-equipped army, and a stiff-necked patriot, he enjoyed poor relations with Gen. Shafter. After the war and Shafter's replacement by Brig. Gen. Leonard Wood, relations improved, and García was persuaded to go to the United States. He received a public welcome in New York, and an interview with President McKinley in Washington. He died suddenly in the latter city, Dec. 11, 1898, at the age of seventy-one. See David F. Trask, *The War with Spain in 1898* (New York: Macmillan, 1981), p. 323.

4. Getting the troops ashore was not easy, and even the start of the operation, getting them off the *St. Paul* into the small boats, was difficult:

> There were many amusing scenes at the gangway ladder when the soldiers were leaving. The sea was a little rough, and the big cutters of the *St. Paul* danced rather lively on the swell. Frequently as a soldier jumped into the boat he did not allow for the motion and went sprawling in the bottom. This was always sufficient excuse for a rousing cheer from his company on the deck above.
>
> There was one fellow whom they called Wiley [Cpl. Charles O. Wiley of Company K, aged twenty-four]—evidently one of the characters of the regiment—whose aversion to water in any form was apparent. Wiley was no longer a youth, and as he stepped on the ladder and nervously grasped the manrope it was evident that Wiley was more afraid of the water than he was of the Spanish or he wouldn't have enlisted. There were loud cries of "Look at Wiley! He never did like water!" from the decks above. Wiley, feeling that he was the center of attention, became more and more nervous as he neared the bottom. There he hesitated. The boat rose and fell. There were shouts of "Now, Wiley; now is your chance!" His foot was raised—he was poised for the leap, but he could not let go of the manrope.
>
> The boat was carried out from the landing several feet by the next swell. The coxswain in charge was becoming impatient at the delay. Wiley's tormentors were becoming more vociferous. Finally in mad despair Wiley gathered himself together and raised his foot; the crowd waited for the leap. Then he put it down again, and the crowd jeered. Wiley could stand it

> no longer. He let go the rope and frantically leaped at the boat. Just then the boat swiftly dropped to the swell, and Wiley brought up in a heap of arms, legs, canteens and haversacks at the bottom, midst a perfect storm of applause from above.
>
> The last to leave was the regimental band and the baggage detail. As they shoved off on the navy tug *Leyden* someone proposed three cheers for the *St. Paul*, and in return three rousing cheers for the Eighth Ohio were given by the sailors. The band played "Auld Lang Syne" and the tug gave a farewell toot. The last of the Eighth Ohio were gone, and not a few lingered at the rail absorbed in revery as they watched the tug disappearing in the distance.

Lt. W. V. N. Powelson, "Ocean Liner *St. Paul* as an Army Transport," *New York Herald*, August 14, 1898 (copy in Hard MSS).

Powelson, incidentally, was an interesting individual who already had played an important part in the war. A young graduate of the Naval Academy, and student of naval architecture, he had been present at the court of inquiry in Havana concerning the sinking of the *Maine*, and testified to his belief that a submerged mine had sunk the battleship. G. J. A. O'Toole, *The Spanish War: An American Epic—1898* (New York: W. W. Norton, 1984), pp. 135-38, 142.

5. "The native Cubans about the town were a sorry lot, all sizes and colors, with nothing to eat and very little to wear; they seemed anxious to work for something to eat, but made very poor workers. We had a large lot of very fat salt pork, which of course had been exposed to the sun and rains, and in consequence had become very soft. I wanted to have it stacked up nicely and got a lot of the fellows to do it. After they had worked a while I allowed each man to take his machete, and cut off a piece about the size of two fists, also gave each a few hardtacks. They were delighted, and the way they waded into that raw, fat pork, was something wonderful to see." Kuhns, "Feeding an Army," pt. 4, *Hotel World*.

6. Col. Hard seems not have understood the difficulties of unloading the Eighth's supplies from the *St. Paul*, dismissing them in a sentence. Capt. Kuhns was more specific:

> I was left on the *St. Paul* with seventy-two men to unload our stores and provisions, a very tedious and difficult operation. In the first place, the property was hard to locate, and often difficult to get, after having been located, as we often had to move great quantities of stores before we could get at ours. The sea being rough it was a laborious task to lower the boxes on the ship's side into the small boats, and notwithstanding the exercise of the greatest care in handling, many were battered to pieces against the ship or dropped into the sea. A great deal of property was lost in this way. Captain Sigsbee secured a small converted yacht, the *Leyden*, to assist, but while this was a help in getting the stores off the *St. Paul* it was a detriment at the other end, as the *Leyden* could not land at Siboney and we were compelled to reload from her to the small boat, this having to be done by hand. The only advantage gained was the saving of about a mile of rowing. I sent about two-thirds of the men ashore to handle the stores, which had to be piled upon the beach. No shelter of any kind was to be provided, every building in the town, save two, having been burned the day we landed, to prevent the spread of yellow fever. We carried a large amount of ammunition, and great difficulty was experienced in landing it from the small boats, the boxes being so heavy.

Pt. 3, ibid. And again:

> The men had to strip and wade right into the water. About four men on each side would hold the boat while the others carried boxes. Many times, in spite of our best efforts, the boats would be beached, and then to get them back into the water was no small task. This work created much amusement for the lookers on. Nearly every time two men would start with a box, a big wave would come up behind them, and over would go men and box. Fully two-thirds of this ammunition had been under water before it was landed; fortunately it was waterproof.

Pt. 4, ibid.

7. The engagement at Las Guásimas on June 24, the first stand of Spanish troops after the American landings at Daiquiri and Siboney, was little more than a skirmish. The Spanish were under orders to retire toward Santiago. Nonetheless it was a serious business, in which Spanish troops stationed themselves along a ridge and could have delayed the Americans, had they tried. American losses were sixteen dead and fifty-two wounded; Spanish losses totaled ten killed and twenty-five wounded. Maj. Gen. Joseph Wheeler was in command, and Col. Leonard Wood's regiment, the Rough Riders, was in the thick of the fighting. Hamilton Fish, Jr., grandson of President Grant's secretary of state, was among the dead. See Frank Freidel, *The Splendid Little War* (Boston: Little, Brown, 1958), pp. 99–117; Jack Cameron Dierks, *A Leap to Arms: The Cuban Campaign of 1898* (Philadelphia: Lippincott, 1970), 89-93; Trask, *The War with Spain in 1898*, pp. 217-24; O'Toole, *The Spanish War*, pp. 269-79.

8. Hard afterward read Gen. Shafter's official report, which remarked that "There was no lack of transportation, for at no time up to the surrender could all the wagons I had be used." He may have told his young Wooster acquaintance, Pvt. Harry L. McClarran, Jr., about Shafter, for McClarran wrote home on July 26 that the commanding general received all the praise in the newspapers that deserved to go to Gen. Wheeler, who did all the work, and that Shafter "has two orderlies fanning him all the time." McClarran MSS, American History Research Center, University of Akron. The reputation of Gen. Shafter during and after the Santiago campaign was not high, probably because of his crusty personality, and also his appearance as cataloged by Col. Hard. Born in Michigan in 1835, he had volunteered at the outset of the Civil War, from which he emerged a brevet brigadier general. He was posted to the West and became a Regular Army brigadier general only in 1897, a fact that accounts for some of the annoyance of his general officer colleagues in 1898. During the campaigning before Santiago he frequently was ill. In retrospect it does not seem that he deserves the blame that contemporaries so generously bestowed, for his entire command was afflicted by fever. As for the claim that he was reckless with the lives of his men, that is difficult to be sure of, for such subordinates as Maj. Gen. Wheeler would have been difficult to restrain, as would the men themselves who, with hardly any military experience, were full of fight. Shafter died in 1906. See *DAB*, s.v. "William Rufus Shafter."

9. From 1895 to 1903, Nelson A. Miles was the army's commanding general, holding the predecessor office to what, after the Army Reorganization Act of 1902, became the office of chief of staff. In this post, in succession to Lt. Gen. John M. Schofield, he proved a failure. As Graham Cosmas has written in *An Army for Empire*, pp. 59–62, "the post of Commanding General required tact, self-effacement, and political sophistication—all qualities he lacked." Miles had shown great promise. Born in Massachusetts in 1839, a much-honored veteran of the Civil War from which he emerged a corps commander at the age of twenty-five, he was commissioned a colonel in the Regular Army in 1866. Gen. Ulysses S. Grant considered him one of the five best officers of the army, and Gen. William T. Sherman (whose niece he married) referred to him as "the only man who amounts to anything." Miles took a large part in the post-1865 campaigns against the Western Indians—the Sioux, Nez Perce, and Apaches. He commanded the federal troops that broke the Pullman strike in 1894. But in Washington his worst qualities came to the fore, and in 1898 he was passed over for command of the Cuba campaign and given the less prestigious task of leading the expedition to Puerto Rico. Appointed lieutenant general in 1901, he retired in 1903, and died in 1925. In addition to the account in Cosmas see the sketch of Miles by a fellow officer and major general in World War I, Charles Dudley Rhodes, *DAB*, s.v. "Nelson A. Miles."

10. Davis was the best-known reporter of his time, and covered six wars: the insurrection against the Spanish in Cuba beginning in 1895, the Greco-Turkish, Spanish-American, Boer, and Russo-Japanese wars, and World War I. Born in 1864, he died in 1916. He produced seven

volumes of war recollections, twelve of short stories, seven novels, and twenty-five plays. His critical biographer wrote that "he dealt mainly with the surface of life, and . . . even his best work will not long endure. He was too facile, too headlong, too obsessed with contemporaneousness, and he unquestionably published too much." *DAB,* s.v. "Richard Harding Davis."

11. The Spanish surrendered in Santiago on July 17. "On Sunday, the seventeenth, in company with Colonel Hard and Lieutenant Colonel Charles Dick, I started to see the San Juan battlefield and if possible to be present in Santiago at the ceremony of the surrender. We had one horse for the three; while one rode the other two walked, except when part of the time we rode double. I quote from a letter written home that evening: 'We went within a mile and a half of Santiago, but were not permitted to go farther without a pass, which we had failed to procure. We were on top of San Juan Hill when the ceremony took place, and with the aid of our field glasses could see the Spanish soldiers marching around and stacking arms.'" Kuhns, "Feeding an Army," pt. 5, *Hotel World.* A force under Gen. Miles left Santiago on July 21 for Puerto Rico, meeting other troops from the American mainland. When the Spanish government concluded a general armistice with the United States on Aug. 12, Miles's troops had overrun most of the island, at a cost of four dead and about forty wounded.

VI Fever

1. The fevers recounted above and in the following pages were signs of malaria, not—as announced at the time—yellow fever. Shafter and his fellow officers, including medical officers on the scene, together with everyone in Washington, military and civil authorities alike, exhibited much confusion over the nature of the troops' fevers. The problem, of course, was the primitive medical knowledge of the time. The men had been told to expect yellow fever in September, and from the outset there was a sense of urgency that the dread disease might overtake Shafter's army. But when malarial cases appeared, and began to multiply very rapidly, these cases soon began to be described as yellow fever. See Cosmas, *An Army for Empire,* pp. 254-57.

2. Altogether, twenty-five men of the Eighth died in Cuba, and after the war the army removed their bodies to the United States. For the Ohio regiment the task of identification was easy, because of bottles and headboards and the custom of burial parties of piling stones on graves to prevent vultures from digging up the bodies. Early in 1899, Col. Hard took charge of the work of removal. "We want all the boys of Ohio to find their final resting place within the borders of the old Buckeye State," he told a reporter. The National Casket Company, he learned, would furnish caskets. "I saw one of the caskets," he said, "and they are not of the cheap order. They are fine cases and have air-tight zinc lining." As he explained the procedure, each casket would contain a rough box, and inside the latter would be dry sawdust "to make shipment absolutely safe." All sides of the box would have stenciled identification, and the stencil itself placed inside. A corps of about a dozen men, selected from the army, individuals who understood the work, was to gather the bodies. Undertakers would accompany them, and different localities would probably follow Ohio's example and send special representatives to make sure no soldier was overlooked. Cubans would do the work of lifting the bodies. *Cleveland Leader* [?], Jan. 2, 1899. Clipping in Hard MSS.

3. Chaplain Campbell wrote home Aug. 6: "We reached camp shortly after noon. I was given a strange, sad welcome on all sides. There was no noise. Quietly, I was told: 'We need you, if ever a chaplain was needed.' There was a hush and silence over the camp; and fear, and heart hunger, and home hunger, that only a soldier in a strange land feels, were written on almost every face. The camp had been stricken with fever. Ten boys had been laid to rest in the little

cemetery, and within forty minutes after my arrival my duty was to conduct the burial service of a mere boy, who had died the night before. . . . " Unidentified newspaper clipping dated Nov. 13, in Col. Hard's papers. The new chaplain must have been effective. According to the diary of Pvt. McClarran, Aug. 7, 1898: "Went to services. It was Rev. Campbell's first but was cut short by rain to the sorrow of all." And again, Aug. 14: " . . . went to church at 4:00 p.m. Chaplain Campbell's first sermon and it was first rate." McClarran MSS.

4. During the Eighth's quarantine its officers communicated directly with President McKinley about the regiment's condition. On July 18, Lt. Col. Dick, perhaps in his office (for which he was still being paid) as secretary of the Republican National Committee, wrote that there were twenty-eight reported cases of yellow fever at Siboney, and twenty among the Rough Riders, that the Eighth was in fine shape but needed to get away. Two days later he said the regiment had only a dozen ill, two seriously, and the men were boiling all water and eating no native fruit. He said four hundred cases of yellow fever had been reported as of that morning, but then everything was called that. Col. Hard wrote on the twenty-fifth that there was no yellow fever, only mountain or thermal fever, that he himself had had a fever for a few days, that there was need to get away. He said he had cabled the president the day before asking for prompt mail delivery—there had been none thus far. All officers, of whatever rank, feared to appeal to Shafter, and someone was trying to keep the truth "regarding the situation" from getting out. "When the true story of the Santiago campaign is written, if it is ever told," opined the colonel, "the people of the United States will be astounded and amazed . . . . [I]t will make the most shameful page in American history." Dick wrote the same day and said the army was approaching an appalling situation, that high-ranking officers had suggested he write, that it was time to get out, with only a few men ill, that some divisions were in trouble, that the First Division of 4,500 men had 1,100 sick, and five hundred serious cases were at Siboney. Dick to McKinley, July 18, 20; Hard to McKinley, July 25; Dick to McKinley, July 25, McKinley MSS, microfilm, series 1, reel 4.

5. Hard much disliked Shafter after his interviews, and willingly picked up the canard that Shafter's principal officers had produced the so-called round robin so as to get action in the War Department. In fact the document did not contain a circle of signatures, and constituted no criticism of the commanding general. The signers had drawn it up to support Shafter, and sent it to Washington with his full knowledge. An enterprising reporter obtained a copy, however, and cabled it home. People there had not been prepared for the situation of the troops in Cuba and its publication created a sensation. It not merely raised a storm of criticism against the War Department but harmed the negotiation for an armistice then in progress with the Spanish government.

6. John C. Bates, born in 1842, was the son of Edward Bates, attorney general in Lincoln's cabinet. A Civil War veteran, he remained in the army, serving in Northwestern posts and along the Mexican border. In 1898 he was commissioned brigadier general and major general of volunteers, later served in the Philippines, and in 1906 became army chief of staff for a few months, with the rank of lieutenant general. He died in 1919. *DAB,* s.v. "John Coalter Bates."

7. After the war a public contention arose over provisioning the army, especially issuance of canned meat, which supposedly was so bad it was not canned but "embalmed." Gen. Miles used the issue to attack the War Department, Secretary Alger, and the McKinley administration. According to Graham Cosmas, the packers "foisted on the Army at least a few bad lots of the meat, cans containing scraps of gristle, pieces of rope, and even dead maggots," but most of it was good. *An Army for Empire,* pp. 284-92. Capt. Kuhns vigorously defended the quality of meat issued in Cuba.

> The canned roast beef, I admit, was far from being as palatable as a "Filet de Boeuf, á la Chateaubriand," but was so far ahead of nothing that my observation led me to believe that the men were reasonably well satisfied with it, although, as a rule, they were not particularly fond of it. At times we had canned corned beef, which was much preferred. I never heard

of "embalmed" beef in Cuba, nor did I ever hear hinted that the meat had been doctored. Some days after we had commenced to draw rations from Santiago, I was informed that I could get fresh meat, and got one or two loads to camp with fair success, but soon discovered that it was not practical. The second load I took out left Santiago before six o'clock in the morning, and did not reach camp until ten o'clock that night, having been exposed to the sun and rain all day. Of course, there was but one thing to be done with that load, and that was to bury it. The roads were so bad, and the creeks so treacherous, that one could never tell how long it would take a wagon to get over that nine miles of road. I examined the fresh beef as it came from the ships at Santiago several times, and all I saw was good; indeed, I thought at the time, remarkably so. After our camp was moved to within two miles of the city, we used the fresh beef, but, of course had no ice, and if it was not used quickly would putrefy.

Kuhns, "Feeding an Army," pt. 6, *Hotel World*.

8. "The patriotic Cuban gentlemen . . . have a very fine club called the 'San Carlos,' and spend much of their time there. At this club light lunch is served at any time, and I noticed that the Cubans were great coffee drinkers; they use very small cups, but drink any number of them during the day. The coffee is exceedingly strong, but well prepared. I do not think any of the Cubans ever saw a large coffee cup, and were much amused to see me pour a cup of coffee into a glass and fill it with hot water." (Ibid.) Brig. Gen. Leonard Wood, late colonel of the Rough Riders, had served in the Regular Army beginning with the Apache campaigns of the 1880s, and after the Spanish-American War became military governor of Santiago and then of all Cuba. He was army chief of staff in 1910-14. During World War I he commanded training divisions, and in the 1920s became governor general of the Philippines. Wood was a close friend of Theodore Roosevelt. A graduate of the Harvard Medical School, he was one of the principal soldiers and administrators of his era. Born in 1860, he died in 1927. See Jack C. Lane, *Armed Progressive: General Leonard Wood* (San Rafael, Calif.; Presidio, 1978).

9. A Regular Army colonel, Henry W. Lawton was born in 1843 and rose from private to lieutenant colonel during the Civil War. Commissioned a second lieutenant in the Regular Army in 1867, he took part in the Indian wars and in 1886—after a 1,300-mile pursuit through the mountains of Arizona and Mexico—captured Geronimo. Serving in Cuba as brigadier general and major general of volunteers, he commanded the Second Division before Santiago, was one of the commissioners to receive the surrender, and became military governor of the city and province. He was killed in the Philippines in 1899. Lawton was "a striking and soldierly figure—six feet four inches tall, erect and well built. He was quick and energetic in manner and speech, a fine organizer, a thoroughly practical field soldier, and a highly competent commander. . . . " *DAB*, s.v. "Henry Ware Lawton."

10. The odyssey of the sick from Sevilla Hill was set out in a letter from Pvt. Arthur C. Johnson of Company B, published in the *Summit County Beacon*, Sept. 1, 1898:

The party consisted of seventy-five men at first, but as the sick were sent forward there were but seventeen in all remaining when the regiment moved on board and of these only seven were sick. Two of these, Sgts. C. H. Cranz and James R. Thomas, were from Company B, and Sgt. Earl Cranz and Arthur Johnson [the writer] the nurses detailed to care for them. James Cole, who was also of the detail, himself fell sick and was sent on to the regiment as soon as he was able to walk the distance. . . .

The doctor mounted one of the men on his mule and sent him posthaste to the city. He returned late in the evening of Wednesday through rain and mud with an army wagon and four mules, to bring the sick at once to Santiago, as the regiment was aboard the *Mohawk* and waiting.

There was no driver with the team and the difficulty was increasing. Being compelled to wait until morning we finally loaded the seven sick men on the wagon and with the baggage made them as comfortable as possible, and started. Three different times through mismanagement of the team the wagon nearly upset and stuck in the streams we were compelled to cross. It was raining; and to cap the climax one mule became sick at the San Juan ford and left the wagon stuck in four feet of rising mud and water. The men worked up to their shoulders in the stream, and finally, with the assistance of another passing team, the wagon was extricated.

We left camp at daybreak, and when the sick were carried into the Red Cross hospital at last, it was three o'clock in the afternoon, having required all that time in making the trip of four and one-half miles, over that awful road.

Sgts. C. H. Cranz and James R. Thomas were admitted to the hospital and will be brought to New York within a very few days on the hospital boat *Olivette,* then waiting in the harbor. The nurses and convalescents who were able went at once to the docks, where Col. Hard and Capt. Maynes were waiting with the tug *Esmeralda,* and going aboard we were soon under the bows of the *Mohawk* which with many other transports was lying in the harbor at quite a distance from the docks.

Very little time was wasted in getting under way. The big vessel swung slowly around and started on her voyage at four o'clock.

VII Aboard the *Mohawk*

1. Capt. Kuhns's account says 1,500 men and 900 mules. "Feeding an Army," pt. 7, *Hotel World.*

2. "I did everything within my power to have the ration used to the best advantage. Every man got all he would eat of that which was provided, which included every article prescribed by regulations. In addition to this, I superintended the making of coffee, and each day after the first supplied one hundred and twenty gallons of soup. Serious complaint [was] made that [the] soup contained insufficient salt, which I admit was true, but it must be remembered that, while canned meats and vegetables furnished for travel rations are properly seasoned, they do not hold sufficient seasoning to carry the amount of water necessary for a palatable soup. I bought all the salt the ship's steward had, and also rice, and barley, but still complaint was made." Ibid.

3. "The rations we drew for this trip had evidently been in Cuba for some time, as we found the hard tack to be in bad condition; some of it wormy and quite a lot of the canned meats were spoiled. Fortunately ten days' rations were drawn, and we found enough of good material to last during the voyage. The spoiled rations were not discovered until we were under way, everything coming on board in boxes." Ibid.

VIII Montauk Point

1. The *Cleveland Leader,* Aug. 31, 1898, headlined THE AWFUL SUFFERING OF THE EIGHTH OHIO. In smaller type it explained: "The story is graphically told by gaunt, hollow-eyed, fever-marked wrecks. Some plain unvarnished truths. Troops fed on wormy hard tack, spoiled tomatoes, and sour beans. Quartered on a deck where a thousand mules had been—too weak to stand the men lay down in filth, and bugs and flies swarmed over them—endured slow torture while the officers dined in luxury."

2. Frank J. Hecker cared for the Eighth's immediate problems, but was a man of much larger talent than Colonel Hard imagined. A Detroit business associate of Secretary Alger, brought into the War Department and given a colonelcy, he had supervised all water transportation for the army. Moving with dispatch, Hecker bought fourteen large steamers for Atlantic operations, including the *Mohawk,* enough to carry 14,000 troops and 7,000 horses and mules. He bought two more steamers especially for the Pacific run to Manila. He also secured a variety of tugs and barges and lighters. All in all he spent over $16,500,000. His work proved invaluable in relieving the immediate shipping shortage and meeting the commitments overseas that came out of the war. See Cosmas, *An Army for Empire,* pp. 218-19.

IX Epilogue

1. *Cleveland Leader,* Aug. 31, 1898.
2. Clipping of unidentified Cleveland paper, Sept. 8, 1898, in Hard MSS.
3. Ibid.
4. *Baltimore Sun,* Sept. 4, 1898.
5. A variant of this tale went as follows: "While in Cuba an Eighth Ohio man, it was said, married a Cuban senorita. For three days he ran the guard line established by the 34th Michigan volunteer regiment, and paid due respect to his bride. On the fourth day he deserted the woman of his choice. She and her father notified the colonel, who lined up in ranks the entire regiment and told the jilted bride to pick out her recreant spouse. Up and down the ranks she went, closely scrutinizing each soldier, but was finally compelled to admit that they all looked alike to her, and the husband escaped detection." *Akron Beacon Journal,* Sept. 18, 1898.
6. *Wooster Daily Republican,* Nov. 17, 1898.
7. *Wooster Evening Journal,* Nov. 18, 1898.
8. *Wooster Daily Republican,* Nov, 17; *Canton News-Democrat,* Nov. 22; *Wooster Evening Journal,* Nov. 22, 1898.
9. *Wooster Evening Journal,* Nov. 22, 1898.
10. Dick left Santiago on Aug. 4 and was detained five days in quarantine, and arrived in Washington on Aug. 14. The purpose of the trip, as he wrote the president, was to "lay before you the condition of the army." But the day he left Santiago orders already were going to Shafter (orders went on Aug. 3–5) to take the troops out. Dick to McKinley, Aug. 14, 1898, McKinley MSS, microfilm, series 1, reel 4.

For Further Reading

The best single volume about the war is by David F. Trask, *The War with Spain in 1898* (New York: Macmillan, 1981). See also the short account by H. Wayne Morgan, *America's Road to Empire: The War with Spain and Overseas Expansion* (New York: Wiley, 1965). For the vicissitudes of the U.S. Army see Jack Cameron Dierks, *A Leap to Arms: The Cuban Campaign of 1898* (Philadelphia: Lippincott, 1970) and especially Graham A. Cosmas, *An Army for Empire: The United States Army in the Spanish-American War* (Columbia, Mo.: University of Missouri Press, 1971). Walter Millis, *The Martial Spirit: A Study of Our War with Spain* (Boston: Houghton Mifflin, 1931), is still worth attention, although marred by commentaries about the war's foolishness. For more recent treatments, as colorful as Millis, see Frank Freidel, *The Splendid Little War* (Boston: Little, Brown, 1958), and G. J. A. O'Toole, *The Spanish War: An American Epic—1898* (New York: Norton, 1984). The precipitating cause of the war, the sinking of the *Maine,* has been carefully examined in John Edward Weems, *The Fate of the Maine* (New York: Holt, 1958), and Hyman Rickover, *How the Battleship Maine was Destroyed* (Washington, D.C.: Naval History Division, Department of the Navy, 1976). The only scholarly study of a military figure is Ronald Spector, *Admiral of the New Empire: The Life and Career of George Dewey* (Baton Rouge: Louisiana State University Press, 1974).

Foreign affairs are in Ernest R. May, *Imperial Democracy: The Emergence of America as a Great Power* (New York: Harcourt Brace Jovanovich, 1961) and the same author's *American Imperialism: A Speculative Essay* (New York: Atheneum, 1968); Walter La Feber, *The New Empire: An Interpretation of American Expansion, 1860–1898* (Ithaca: Cornell University Press, 1963); Paolo E. Coletta, ed., *Threshold to American Internationalism: Essays on the Foreign Policies of William McKinley* (New York: Exposition, 1970); David Healy, *US Expansionism* (Madison: University of Wisconsin Press, 1970); Milton Plesur, *America's Outward Thrust* (DeKalb, Ill.: Northern Illinois University Press, 1971); Charles S. Campbell, Jr., *The Transformation of American Foreign Relations* (New York: Harper and Row, 1976); Richard

Bradford, *The Virginius Affair* (Boulder, Colo.: Colorado Associated University Press, 1980); Robert L. Beisner, *From the Old Diplomacy to the New: 1865–1900,* 2d ed. (Arlington Heights, Ill.: Harlan Davidson, 1986); and Joyce Goldberg, *The Baltimore Affair* (Lincoln, Nebr.: University of Nebraska Press, 1986).

For biographies of principal figures other than military men see Margaret Leech, *In the Days of McKinley* (New York: Harper, 1959), and H. Wayne Morgan, *William McKinley and His America* (Syracuse: Syracuse University Press, 1963); also Tyler Dennett, *John Hay: From Poetry to Politics* (New York: Dodd, Mead, 1933); Kenton J. Clymer, *John Hay: The Gentleman as Diplomat* (Ann Arbor: University of Michigan Press, 1975); and John Braeman, *Albert J. Beveridge* (Chicago: University of Chicago Press, 1971). W. A. Swanberg has analyzed the rivalry of the two principal newspaper proprietors in New York City, *Citizen Hearst: A Biography of William Randolph Hearst* (New York: Scribner's, 1961), and *Pulitzer* (New York: Scribner's, 1967).

The witty disgust of the fictitious critic of American imperialism, Mr. Dooley, is in Finley Peter Dunne's *Mr. Dooley: In Peace and in War* (Boston: Small, Maynard, 1899). Robert L. Beisner, *Twelve Against Empire: The Anti-Imperialists, 1898—1900* (New York: McGraw-Hill, 1968), and Frank Freidel's essay in *Dissent in Three American Wars* (Cambridge, Mass.: Harvard University Press, 1970), cover the Spanish-American War. The distinguished Swedish scholar, Goeran Rystad, in *Ambiguous Imperialism* (Stockholm: Esselte Studium, 1973), shows the peculiar mixture of politics and imperialism in the presidential election of 1900. Paul H. Buck, *The Road to Reunion: 1865–1900* (Boston: Little, Brown, 1937), sets out a notable result of the war, the consolidation of American nationalism.

Index